CAMBRIDGE LIBRARY COLLECTION

Books of enduring scholarly value

East and South-East Asian History

This series focuses on East and South-East Asia from the early modern period to the end of the Victorian era. It includes contemporary accounts of European encounters with the civilisations of China, Japan and South-East Asia from the time of the Jesuit missions and the East India companies to the Chinese revolution of 1911.

The Closing Events of the Campaign in China

This 1843 work by naval officer Granville Gower Loch (1813–53) is based on his journal of the capture of Chinkiang (Zhenjiang) in July 1842, the last major battle of the First Opium War. Covering not only military and diplomatic activity, the work also contains Loch's colourful descriptions of the region's landscape, architecture, commerce, people and customs. Having been promoted to captain in August 1841, Loch had gone to China as a volunteer and aide-de-camp to General Sir Hugh Gough (1779–1869). Following service in the West Indies, he was killed on a mission in Burma during the Second Anglo-Burmese War. A monument was erected to his memory in St Paul's Cathedral. One of his brothers, Henry Brougham Loch (1827–1900), also later served under Gough and his *Personal Narrative of Occurrences during Lord Elgin's Second Embassy to China* (1869) has been reissued in this series.

T0370696

Cambridge University Press has long been a pioneer in the reissuing of out-of-print titles from its own backlist, producing digital reprints of books that are still sought after by scholars and students but could not be reprinted economically using traditional technology. The Cambridge Library Collection extends this activity to a wider range of books which are still of importance to researchers and professionals, either for the source material they contain, or as landmarks in the history of their academic discipline.

Drawing from the world-renowned collections in the Cambridge University Library and other partner libraries, and guided by the advice of experts in each subject area, Cambridge University Press is using state-of-the-art scanning machines in its own Printing House to capture the content of each book selected for inclusion. The files are processed to give a consistently clear, crisp image, and the books finished to the high quality standard for which the Press is recognised around the world. The latest print-on-demand technology ensures that the books will remain available indefinitely, and that orders for single or multiple copies can quickly be supplied.

The Cambridge Library Collection brings back to life books of enduring scholarly value (including out-of-copyright works originally issued by other publishers) across a wide range of disciplines in the humanities and social sciences and in science and technology.

The Closing Events of the Campaign in China

The Operations in the Yang-Tze-Kiang, and Treaty of Nanking

GRANVILLE GOWER LOCH

CAMBRIDGE
UNIVERSITY PRESS

CAMBRIDGE
UNIVERSITY PRESS

University Printing House, Cambridge, CB2 8BS, United Kingdom

Published in the United States of America by Cambridge University Press, New York

Cambridge University Press is part of the University of Cambridge.

It furthers the University's mission by disseminating knowledge in the pursuit of
education, learning and research at the highest international levels of excellence.

www.cambridge.org
Information on this title: www.cambridge.org/9781108061384

© in this compilation Cambridge University Press 2013

This edition first published 1843
This digitally printed version 2013

ISBN 978-1-108-06138-4 Paperback

This book reproduces the text of the original edition. The content and language reflect
the beliefs, practices and terminology of their time, and have not been updated.

Cambridge University Press wishes to make clear that the book, unless originally published
by Cambridge, is not being republished by, in association or collaboration with, or
with the endorsement or approval of, the original publisher or its successors in title.

THE

CLOSING EVENTS

OF THE

CAMPAIGN IN CHINA:

THE

OPERATIONS IN THE YANG-TZE-KIANG;

AND

TREATY OF NANKING.

BY

CAPT. GRANVILLE G. LOCH,

ROYAL NAVY.

LONDON:

JOHN MURRAY, ALBEMARLE STREET.

MDCCCXLIII.

PREFACE.

ANXIOUS to see China and witness the operations then proceeding there, I took the opportunity that offered of my return from active service in the Mediterranean to apply in December, 1841, to the Admiralty for leave to join the Expedition, which was most kindly granted, and I embarked for a passage on board H. M. S. Dido by the invitation of her captain the Hon. H. Keppel, my old and esteemed friend.

When we joined the force at the mouth of the Yang-tze-kiang, I was invited by Vice-Admiral Sir William Parker to live with him; and I take this opportunity to express my gratitude to him for his unvaried kindness, as also to Sir Hugh Gough, who permitted me to act as his extra aide-de-camp whenever the army landed, and not

A 3

less to Sir Henry Pottinger, who afforded me the same opportunity that he himself possessed of meeting and observing the Chinese authorities, with whom we came in contact during the period of the negotiations.

While I was with the Expedition I kept a journal, and this volume is the result of it.

After the treaty was signed, I proceeded to Calcutta in the H. C. S. Tenasserim, the vessel sent with the despatches to Lord Ellenborough, announcing the conclusion of the war and the treaty which had been agreed upon.

Desirous of seeing something of the British possessions in India, I visited the three presidencies, therefore did not reach England until the end of March, which circumstance has delayed the publication of this book three months longer than I could have wished.

During the period of our short stay, after the capture of the city of Chin-kiang-foo, I had no opportunity of examining, with any degree of accuracy, its extended suburbs, or the course of the Great Canal; but I have been so fortunate as to receive some valuable observations from Captain

the Hon. Fred. Grey, who was left there as senior
naval officer pending the negotiations which succeeded the treaty of Nanking : these he has kindly
permitted me to insert, and they will be found
in the APPENDIX.

CONTENTS.

CHAPTER I.

CHAP. II.

CHAP. III.

CHAP IX.

CHAP. X.

CHAP. XI.

CHAP. XII.

CHAP. XIII.

APPENDIX.

TO THE BINDER.

The map of the Yang-tze-kiang *to face* page 1.

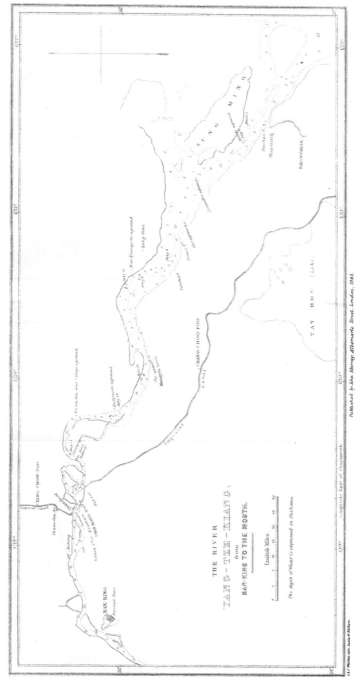

The material originally positioned here is too large for reproduction in this reissue. A PDF can be downloaded from the web address given on page iv of this book, by clicking on 'Resources Available'.

THE CLOSING EVENTS

OF THE

CAMPAIGN IN CHINA,

&c.

CHAPTER I.

LATE on the evening of the 26th of April, 1842, we rounded Java Head and entered the Straits of Sunda, the great western entrance to the China Sea.

Our passage so far had been prosperous; we sailed from Plymouth Sound on the 23d of January, and anchored in Simon's Bay on the 21st of March. To our surprise, we there found Lord Saltoun and his troops. They had left England five weeks before us, and we may attribute our good fortune in overtaking them to the light and variable winds they experienced between

B

Rio de Janeiro and the Cape. They sailed the forenoon after our arrival, and four days before us : it remains to be seen whether we have gained stronger and better winds since leaving the Cape by steering a parallel latitude farther south, and continuing it farther to the eastward than the usual track vessels follow, or Horsburgh recommends. Hitherto our daily runs have been particularly good, having accomplished a distance of 5752 miles in 31 days.

Wednesday, 27th of April. — I rose before sunrise to enjoy a sight that is seen to greater advantage in this climate than in any other, and to appreciate fully the satisfactory sensation of a ship sailing in smooth seas after an antarctic passage.

The water was as little disturbed as an inland lake, — only slightly rippled by a six-knot breeze, wafting " the spicy gales of the sweet South " to our up-turned noses. No pack of fox-hounds were ever more anxious to sniff Reynard's tail than we were to inhale the smell of the land.

For the last few days the winds have been light and variable, and the temperature extremely oppressive; to us particularly so, who only a week before had snow upon our decks.

This is the month of change, the month in which the easterly winds and fair weather are ushered in by lightning and tempests, violent tornadoes, and deluges of rain. After a short period the heavy clouds disappear; the atmosphere expands; the air becomes pure and refreshing; nature revives, and the earth is once more clad with beautiful verdure. In September, nature begins to droop; the breezes become light and fitful; the strongest are oppressed with languor; clouds assemble in huge masses, which, in October, burst forth in thunder, lightning, and heavy squalls. These squalls frequently ripen into gales; and thus the rainy S. W. monsoon sets in, continuing until the sun is again within the tropic of Cancer.

This is the climate of the islands to the south and upon the equator. The great continent of Asia alters the direction of these winds. The summer monsoon of Java and Sumatra is N. E.; it is N. W. over China and Hindostan; in like manner the S. W. monsoon of the Archipelago is the S. E. of the mainland.

During the day three canoes came off with some unripe fruit, fowls, and paroquets; they were manned by Malays, all ready and anxious to take every advantage in disposing of their commodities. The canoes are scooped from single trees and finished in the rudest manner. It is strange how much the natives of the South Sea

Islands excel in neatness and ingenuity these people, who, in some of the useful arts, are their superiors.

We skirted the verdant shores, which were every where beautiful, exhibiting all the rich variety of tropical vegetation; — the teak, owing a borrowed fragrance and bloom to the parasitical plants that clung to it; the gigantic suren, dying within the embrace of a creeper larger than itself; the palm and the valued cocoa nut; the bamboo and the betel nut; the sago palm of Amboyna, and its sister in produce the *Sagurus rumpnii*; the wax and the cotton tree, and other plants supplying every want to a lazy race; and in the arid spots, we learned, that the pitcher plant, *Nepenthes distillatoria*, is found, with its beautiful provision for securing and retaining sufficient moisture for its support under an equatorial sun.

The famous upas, or poison tree, also flourishes here, distinguished by its straight and stately stem rising to the height of seventy or eighty feet; too noble a vegetable, one would suppose, to have ever obtained so bad a reputation.

We were also told of that fearful valley within which no living creature can exist; and a story of a poor convict, who, having escaped from Batavia, had, in his anxiety to elude pursuit, overlooked the dangerous vicinity, and perished within its fatal precincts.

At sunset we shaped our course to the northward. The " Button " and the " Cap " (two small round islands) were far astern, and Batavia, the old queen of the East, where Chinamen pay a tax to wear their pig-tails, far on our starboard quarter.

30*th of April.* — This morning we sighted the island of Banca, and are now running between its shores and those of Sumatra. Pirates and a colony of Chinese tin miners are, I believe, the only inhabitants of the former island, and have, from long practice and industry, arrived at great proficiency in their separate pursuits. Stretching from north to south, we saw on our left the low coast of Sumatra, covered by a continuous forest to the water's edge, which affords shelter to a greater variety of savage animals than perhaps exists in any other country. The single and double horned rhinoceros, the elephant, and a tiger whose strength and ferocity are said to be superior to those of the better known native of Bengal, are amongst the largest. Numbers of people are annually carried off by the latter animal; but still the simple natives as frequently endeavour to propitiate them by offerings of fruit and flowers as they do to destroy them by energetic means.

I believe no sea within the tropics contains so large a family of *Cetacea* as the Eastern Archipelago. Perhaps the most peculiar is the *Dugong*. Its body is bulky, tapering to a broad horizontal tail; instead of fins, it has two webbed paws, armed with talons; its head in shape is very peculiar, and its mouth is furnished with browsing teeth. Its food consists entirely of herbage, which it crops at the bottom of the sea. In size it varies from ten to twenty feet in length, and the flesh resembles young beef, and is highly appreciated by the Malays. The females are strongly attached to their young, and allow themselves to be taken if their offspring are destroyed. They utter sharp and plaintive cries, and are said to shed tears, which are carefully preserved by these most unsophisticated cut-throats.

The Malays, pre-eminently superstitious, even amongst nations remarkable for such a tendency, have numerous legendary stories of the wonderful qualities of many of this tribe of fish; they have obtained a supernatural connection, in their simple imaginations, with many of the sounds and appearances that arise from natural causes amid the wild and beautiful scenery by which they are surrounded. While gliding in their swift *prohas* among their romantic islands, now through the bright moonlight, and now within the deep shadows cast by each wood and headland, every faint echo, the flutter of a startled bird, or growl of savage beast, even the fall of a distant paddle on the calm sea, are not unlikely at such a moment to acquire a mysterious import.

6th of May. — For the last few days we have been running between patches of beautiful islands covered with fine trees, literally embedded in dense and luxuriant underwood. Numerous roots of huge aloes and palms, long bamboos and branches, carried out by the currents from the rivers of Sumatra, have been daily drifting past. They will doubtless accumulate, as we have remarked, in these seas; ground in shoal water, and form a deposit around them; and from this nucleus Nature will cause vegetation to extend her territory.

Yesterday we saw for the first time two Malay *prohas* full of men: I suspect they disliked our appearance as much as a pickpocket does that of a police-officer.

To-day we are in sight of the flag-staff close to Singapore; and if the light air increases, shall hear from old England before nightfall, and also, I trust, a great deal about the Chinese war. A steamer and five or six large ships are in sight, and we are in a state of great expectation; it would not be easy to describe the mingled feelings of anxiety and hope that at such a moment assail a man.

Saturday, 7th of May. — Last night the wind fell, and we were obliged to anchor within a few miles of the port — a most tantalizing occurrence. The transports we saw in the morning had to do the same; so the Captain sent a boat to gain intelligence. These four vessels contain the last of the detachment of 5000 men despatched from India for China. We heard of Lord Auckland's return; of the Ning-po business, and of the increasing obstinacy of the Chinese; and Keppel learned what justly pleased him much — that the Dido was the first ship out of a batch of five men-of-war that left England five, and some even six, weeks before us.

We anchored in this fine harbour about noon in the centre of a fleet of merchant ships.

On the crest of a round hill topping the town, free from jungle and ornamented with nutmeg and other trees, and covered with a compact green sward, worthy of England, stands the governor's handsome bungelow. At the hill's base, on the flat and even ground in front and to the right, extend the houses of our luxurious Eastern merchants — spacious buildings, with fine Roman Doric porticoes, and separated from each other by inclosed gardens. Beyond these appear the humble dwellings of the Chinese colonists skirting the edge of the dense jungle, acres of which are annually cleared, making way for spice plantations, which richly repay the industrious proprietors.

The unvaried luxuriance of vegetation, although very pleasing at first, after some time becomes tiresome. The eye longs for a clear expanse, or the abrupt interruption of a rugged crag. Here there is merely a diversity of gentle hills and shallow dales, all alike clothed with the same thick foliage.

Well-made roads now intersect the island in different directions; and they, indeed, in conjunction with every other improvement, have been planned and executed through the indefatigable exertions of the clever and energetic Governor, Mr. Bonham.

When the British flag was first hoisted by Sir Stamford Raffles in 1819, the population did not exceed 200 souls. In 1820 the numbers had increased to 10,000, principally Chinese; and now the trade (as Lord Jocelyn has correctly stated) is equal to that of Bombay, and the population, consisting of Europeans, Chinese, Malays, Bengalees, Arabs, Buggis, and others, is nearly 30,000.

Singapore is a free port, which is a pity, for a light harbour due would not prevent vessels from coming to a place of such commercial importance, and would more effectually defray the expenses of the straits, and enable the Governor to prosecute

many projected improvements, which, from a paucity of funds, he has been obliged to defer.

At day-dawn, when the sky receives its first
bright tints from the rising sun, and the morning
mist yet shrouds the marshes and hangs about
the damp verdure, the harbour is alive with boats
and resounding with the noisy hum of awakened
crowds; — the long low canoe of the Malay, pro-
pelled by twenty or thirty paddles, each stroke
accompanied by their peculiar cry; punts, the
undoubted progeny of the mother junks, conveying to the shore the Chinese mariner with his
fan and umbrella; the sanpans, with their clean
matted seats and plantain-leaf awnings, waiting
for passengers, and promiscuously manned by the
Hindoo, the Moor, the Malay or the Arab, the
wild native of Borneo or Amboyna, Madura or
the more independent and manly inhabitant of
Bali; the unwieldy junk herself, with painted eyes,
which are presumed to guide it in safety clear of
shoals and dangers, its large masts without rigging, mat sail, high-peaked stern (not unlike ours
of the fifteenth century) bedaubed with flying dragons, painted devils, and proverbs, and the poop
entirely occupied by the indispensable jos, dis-
gorging scores of chattering Chinese; boats laden
with fruit of every description, amongst which pine-
apples predominate, arriving from distant creeks,

ready for the morning market; and the light fishing canoe, with its patient occupant, who will sit
for hours under the shade of his light grass hat,
are amongst the many novelties that attract the
attention of the stranger.

I went on shore with Captain Keppel to call
upon the Governor. We found him at his office,
a large building near the beach; he received his
old friend Keppel most heartily. His active
duties, he says, have greatly accumulated since
the commencement of the Chinese war, and it
is lucky for the naval service that there is so
excellent a manager to supply their demands.

In the evening we relanded to dine with Mr.
Bonham. A palankin drawn by a spirited little
Timour poney, not larger than a Shetlander, conveyed us up the ascent at an active trot: the very
pretty approach to the house, winding round the
east side of the hill and flanked by nutmeg groves
interspersed with some fine timber, is kept in very
excellent order. White jackets and a punkar,
open doors and a free current of air, made the
temperature delightful.

The house commands a fine view of the town
and adjacent country. The former, although built
on a marsh and surrounded by vegetation, is very
healthy, owing to the sea covering the lower
ground at every tide, and thus preventing putre-

faction, which would inevitably ensue from the great heat, if the water was not so regularly renewed.

I was glad to hear that the war has not destroyed the confidence of the Chinese traders, and that the same number of junks continue to arrive, and as richly laden as before. When it is considered how defenceless these valuable vessels are, and that they are generally sailing within sight of numerous little islands, separated by winding channels, yet unsurveyed, and containing creeks and harbours unknown to and screened from the observation of the passing vessel, it is surprising that so few acts of plunder are committed by the Malays, many tribes of whom regard these seas theirs by right of prior possession, and a black mail exacted in their way as lawful taxation. Such exactions they do not consider piracy, nor do they regard them otherwise than did our old borderers their frequent forays. We may hear eventually of some flower of Battan, like the one of Yarrow, displaying a crease instead of spurs on an empty dish.

Alligators abound in every inlet; tigers in the jungle. It was only the other day that one of the former capsized a canoe with its tail, and devoured the proprietor; and about the same time an Indian was carried away by one of the latter while walking on the road close to the town. I was informed on good authority that upwards of forty persons are annually destroyed by these savage beasts, which, singular to say, did not exist on the island of Singapore before we formed settlements there.

8th of May. — I drove through the town this morning with Keppel. The principal proprietors and inhabitants are Chinese : there are streets full of Chinese blacksmiths — fine athletic fellows ; others, of shoemakers and tailors ; and some containing open booths, under canvas awnings, resembling the Persian and Turkish bazaars.

I understand that our celestial subjects here do not treat us with the same outward respect practised by their brethren of Java towards their more tyrannical masters, the Dutch. Here, they never think of letting fall their tails (which, for greater convenience, they wear twisted round their heads) when they speak to you. In China, such an omission is considered as great an insult as it would be in England to enter a room with a hat on ; in Batavia, they not only drop their tails, but stand or squat until Mynheer passes. What struck me particularly was to see employed in common use the various (and to our habits inconvenient) utensils which are in England considered mere curiosities or ornaments, as, for instance, the small china tea-cup and cover, large

glazed paper lantern, and porcelain stool, chopsticks, painted umbrella, glass cloth shirts as fine
as cambric, paper soled shoes, and china jars.

Drove to the jos-house, so well described by
Lord Jocelyn. It is built close to the sea-shore,
in the centre of the Chinese quarter of the town ;
the materials were brought from China for the purpose. It is dedicated to Fo. The outer gates conduct to an open court, neatly tiled and surrounded
by a verandah, under which the embroidered silk
canopies of procession appropriate to the various
idols are arranged. On the beams, stone pillars,
cornices, and wood-work, insects and flowers,
birds and monsters are carved, with depth and
boldness, in every variety of grotesque form.
The corners and gable ends, curving upwards,
are surmounted by porcelain dragons with forked
and gaily coloured tails ; the roof is covered with
glazed tiles made of the same material, but of
a coarser texture, and underneath the projecting
edge, upon a white china belt, flowers and
creepers are exquisitely embossed and coloured.

In the midst of the temple, behind the high
altar, and placed between a blue and red devil,
each the size of life, sits an image of the Tien-
How, or Queen of Heaven — a most ungainly
idol. At the feet of this image are a number of
little devils, each fronted by its pot full of

incense sticks. The devotees seek for the protection of a grinning elf of sandal wood, or
endeavour to propitiate some favourite idol of
porcelain, much after the fashion and practice
among the most superstitious of the followers of
the Romish Church : as Père Intorcetta said, it
seemed as if the Devil had run a race with the
Jesuits to China, and, having got the start of
them, had contrived these things for their mor-
tification.

CHAP. II.

WE sailed from Singapore on the afternoon of the
11th of May, leaving the Rattlesnake and Serpent,
two of our outstripped and crestfallen vanguard,
actively employed completing provisions and water.
When about five miles from the harbour, we passed
within hail of H. M. frigate Thalia, Captain C.
Hope.   He, like the rest, had experienced lighter
winds by keeping a lower latitude.

In the evening we heard, for the third time
since we entered the Archipelago, an extraordinary
noise under the ship's quarters and round her
stern.   It resembled the buzzing of a multitude
of bees, and caused a tremulous motion, which was
distinctly felt by placing the hand on the vessel's
side.   The profound among us speculated upon
the phenomenon, and reasoned most learnedly on
every ideal probability.   One conjectured that

we were grinding over the top shoots of a coral forest; another, that shoals of sucking-fish had mistaken us for a shark; some, that it might be caused by myriads of hissing serpents (I may mention that yellow and black snakes are very numerous in these seas); and some surmised that we were cutting through floating spawn : but the water was free from any phosphoric sparkle, and notwithstanding the varieties of opinion as to its cause, the noise was sufficiently loud to induce the carpenter on its first occurrence to leave his bed and sound the well.

I have since ascertained that it arose from shoals of a large fish peculiar to these seas called the " drumming fish." They make themselves distinctly heard while passing under the bottom of the ship, even at the depth of seven fathoms.

Instead of the steady S. W. monsoon, which we had reason to expect, we encountered light and variable winds, with rain and squalls occa-sionally. At daylight on the 30th of May we sighted land, and ran between two islands of the Lema string.

The first appearance of a hostile shore must always excite a feeling of strong interest. The approach to China, hitherto so little known, in-creased if possible such sensations. Every feature and object on these conical and grass-covered islands of sandstone formation, surrounded by numerous little coves affording safe harbours for fleets of fishing-junks, was examined with more curiosity than its appearance or importance could otherwise have called forth, and the mean huts that occasionally appeared planted on the declivities were peered at by at least twenty glasses, which the quickly repeated cry of " land in sight" brought on deck.

The scenery reminded me forcibly of that of the N. W. coast of Scotland; and if, instead of vessels with mat sails, painted bows, and high trelliced sterns, there had been compact boats, with well-set tanned canvas spread to the breeze, the association would have been complete.

Upwards of 300 large junks passed us, standing out to sea to pick up their night nets. They average about twenty-five tons, and are peopled by entire families of men, women, and children, many of whom have never been on *terra firma*.

About noon we entered the channel of Hong-Kong, and made our number to H. M. ship Blenheim, 72, Captain Sir Thomas Herbert.

We anchored in the midst of men-of-war and transports, in a port where, a few short months before, ships were scarcely ever seen. Along the shore, and scattered over the breast of mountains rising to the height of 1500 feet, were wharfs and extensive stores, forts and magazines, streets of huts and commodious houses, a bazaar and a market place, besides some comfortable bungelows and handsome country-houses, belonging to the public functionaries, built at considerable elevations, to command fresh air and a fine view. Ten months before, when Sir Henry Pottinger first landed, he lived in a pitched tent!

Then three small villages contained the entire population, amounting to about 4000 ; now there are upwards of 12,000 souls in our new town alone, and the great difficulty is, to restrain the rapid increase in proportion to the gradual advancement of the colony. As much as 6000*l.* has been already received during the last year from the sale and lease of lands, and hundreds of desirable lots are marked out, which will be eagerly purchased at a high price when people become fully aware that government will guarantee its powerful protection.

It has many advantages over Macao, although there are several who advocate the superiority of the latter place. Doubtless an old established settlement has its benefits at first, and its closer proximity to Canton secures a gain of time; but this is more than balanced by the superior and safer anchorage of Hong-Kong, and the greater facility we shall have in maintaining a strict obedience to our rule, and greater ease in defending it against attacks.

1st of June. — I left the ship at four o'clock in the morning, with Keppel and a small party, to attend Major C——, the principal magistrate, on an official tour of inspection throughout the island; we were rather late, so he had preceded us. We missed the better path, and had to scramble up the face of the steep and rather high mountain, — an effort which, after our four months' cruise, pumped all the breath out of our bodies. Fine green fern and rich grass clothed the entire surface, and would do capitally to fatten sheep and cattle. When we at last reached the summit, we could see the sea on both sides of the island, and a beautiful and heart-stirring sight was the bay below, in which floated our squadron, containing a portion of the brave band sent to invade the largest empire in the world.

Half way down the narrow and precipitous valley, we saw our good friend the Major seated, surrounded by some soldiers and Chinese servants waiting our approach. We accordingly made the best of our way, and found it no easy matter to stop our *way* when our sea-accustomed legs had fairly gathered impetus. I think nothing is more painful than a rapid descent after a fagging ascent; however, some cold tea the Major had in readiness quickly revived us, and on we pressed.

A stream, as like a Highland burn as possible, bounded over the rocks, leaving small basins at every turn until it reached an expanse of ground near the bottom of the valley, where its clear waters were turned into muddy paddy fields. The path now wound round a tongue of land to the left into a small dell, where there were a few houses built in a line. The patriarch and ruler of this community was standing foremost, ready to receive us. This universal custom of acknowledging the superiority of age has been recognised by us throughout the island; and it is agreeable to see so amiable a usage in practice among the most lawless orders of the Chinese, which these islanders are. In this little village they were exclusively employed in agriculture.

The road was shaded here and there by a species of Scotch fir common in Spain and Portugal; shrubs of wild pomegranate, pine-apple, and the mangoe, but in no great abundance, grew by the sides of the several rivulets. We walked eastward along the southern shore to Titam Bay, were it was once proposed our port should be; but although a considerable harbour, the south-west Monsoon raises a disagreeable swell, and might, when it blew hard, be difficult for ships to work out against.

At the head of this bay, the principal village, Chuck-ni-wan, is situated, — a great resort for fishing-junks, which are generally manned by the most lawless ruffians. The unprotected inhabitants frequently suffer from their depredations.

As this village was the post of importance, the magistrate assumed all his dignity, and paraded all his power. He marched in front; we, the guests, followed, and the soldiers and servants brought up the rear. The little children stood with their fingers in their mouths as we passed; the men looked stupid, and the women inquisitive; and thus on we went. But, unfortunately, the road was narrow; houses to the left, the sea close at hand to the right, and at a corner, tied by a rope from a post to an iron ring through its nostrils, stood a small wild mountain cow, which, as soon as we approached, by a vigorous onset broke its tether, and charged straight for the proper person of the magistrate, who made the best use of his activity for some distance, and at last, by an agile leap over an aloe hedge, planted himself in an old woman's garden, — the owner, I believe, of the frantic beast, — who, losing sight of the Major's judicial dignity, only remembered the trouble likely to attend the recovery of her cow, and gave

it him with the ability and heartiness of all old
women of every country, when they are inclined
to vituperate. We did not visit the elders *this*
time, but passed on to the bed of a mountain tor-
rent, well shaded with trees, where we found a substantial breakfast ready prepared.

After a siesta for a couple of hours, our portion
of the party shook hands with Major C——,
and followed a guide on our return home. We
ascended a sufficiently steep hill to the summit,
and here the north side presented a bank of brushwood descending to a level, called the " Happy
Valley," spread over with paddy fields, except
at certain spots where there were cottages surrounded by indifferent gardens. A good road is
in progress of construction along the shore, and a
cut of some depth through an intervening hill is
nearly completed. We were surprised to see
wharfs and foundations for extensive storehouses
laid with a fine grey granite, and wrought with a
finish that would reflect credit upon a London
mason. They were private property.

It is the general opinion that when the merchants make Hong-Kong their place of residence,
it will, being a free port, attract the shipping of
all nations, and consequently transfer the principal trade from Macao, and the Chinese will
then become the carriers to and from Canton.

Early on the 3d, I made one of a party that went in the H. C. S. Hoogly to Macao. Our course lay between islands and past headlands not differing in feature from the Lema islands. Upon almost every projecting promontory, fisher-men's huts were built, and a bamboo windlass fastened to heave up large square nets spread upon stretchers or beams. They were worked much upon the principle of a drawbridge; the inner ends moored by anchors, the outer fastened to the ropes round the windlass, which lowered them down or hove them up at pleasure.

After a longer passage than we expected, we sighted Macao and the shipping in the outer roadstead. Our small draught of water enabled us to anchor close to the shore, when we were in an instant surrounded by squat, oval-bottomed punts, pulled by specimens of the fair sex. The Chinese woman utters a clacking sound peculiar to herself, and employs her tongue with a volu-bility and a perseverance impossible to surpass. These jays—these unplumed paroquets—lauded the qualities of their respective barks, and de-preciated those of their companions, until we were but too glad to stop their clamour by becoming their customers.

The bay opposite the town forms a crescent; a handsome causeway girds the shore, and protects the old Hongs, governor's house, forts, stores, and public buildings, facing the sea : a hill rises at the back, on which are several churches and monasteries.   The Chinese dwellings cover its southern flank.

The aspect of Macao strongly impresses the beholder with the idea of power departed, — the feeling so constantly associated with the appearance of all Portuguese colonies.   The Chinese exercise a *surveillance* over the Portuguese highly degrading, and restrict their force to 300 indifferent troops.

The lower orders were better dressed and cleaner than I expected to find them, and withal civil enough.   I was disappointed in the shops ; they were small, and built of wood; the lower rooms open to, and on a level with, the streets ; the upper are low dens, badly constructed and very dirty.

We saw them painting representations of some of the late actions, and tracing charts of Chusan and the river Yang-tze-kiang from some of our recent surveys, which will enable the Fan-kweis to sail with safety " in their inner waters." What will not the Chinese do for money ?   They are curious beings : with an outward placidity of temper, and the good humour of amiable people, they possess the hardness of heart and unforgiving

c

nature of the Moor. From all that I hear, *as a nation* they are without virtue, deep feeling, or dignity of character. Sir Thomas Herbert told me, that after battering down forts and houses, and killing hundreds at Amoy, the boats of the Chinese were alongside his ship with supplies, before the guns were secured, to obtain what they prize before any good sentiment or moral obligation — profit and gain.

It is this greed for money which induces them, for so small a bribe as three quarters of a dollar per head, during a truce or amnesty, to kidnap every straggler, and murder every poor sailor or soldier whom they can entice away from camp by fair words or deceitful promises. I grieve to say that many atrocities have been lately perpetrated worthy of the savage cruelty of the robber Procrustes. At Ningpo a marine was kidnapped, and for some time was treated with apparent kindness. In a letter he wrote to a comrade, he expressed his gratitude and surprise at their good nature; the next day his mangled body floated down the river, the sinews torn from the flesh, and the ears and the eyelids cut off. About the same time a sentinel at one of the gates stopped two Chinamen carrying a heavy bundle slung between them on a stick; notwithstanding their remonstrances, he stopped them, and discovered a fellow soldier bound and gagged. The culprits were seized, and sent to Hong-Kong to work in chains.

We may say that the town of Macao was first founded in 1537, by the Portuguese, when they erected sheds to dry some goods destined for tribute, which had been damaged in a storm. These sheds very soon grew into substantial buildings, and albeit such audacious presumption at first drew from the mandarins menaces and threats of extermination, a well-applied bribe soothed their ire; fortifications were raised, and fear connived at further encroachment. They however have never been independent of the Chinese government; a rent paid annually confirmed their vassalage, and a resident mandarin inquisitor, beside ruling the Chinese settlers, takes cognizance of, and reports the proceedings of the Portuguese.

In 1612 they were prohibited from building new houses or repairing old — a corrupt enactment which emanated from the viceroy of Canton for the purpose of exacting an additional revenue by the sale of special permits, and also as a warning to the insolent and rapacious barbarians that they must only depend upon the compassion of the " Son of Heaven " for their support and existence.

In 1580 Macao was declared a republic by its inhabitants. In 1582, by invitation, they ac-

knowledged themselves subjects of the Spanish
monarch, and continued to submit to the Spanish
rule until 1641.

In 1622, and again in 1627, the Dutch attacked the town, and were each time repulsed
with severe loss.

When the Manchow Tartars captured Canton in
1650, the Portuguese again degraded their country
for the sake of gain, by bending the knee of vassalage to the Tartar viceroy.

The Emperor twice offered to make Macao the
general emporium of foreign commerce, and the
offer was twice refused by its short-sighted and
narrow-minded rulers, who were afraid of facili-
tating the progress of other nations to wealth
from the Chinese trade through their port. Macao
was then rich and prosperous; it began to decline from that period.

Macao declared in favour of Don Miguel, and
on his accession sent him a considerable sum of
money.

This colony has never been an incumbrance to
the mother country; it has always maintained
itself, and has in several instances been able to
send presents and remittances to its kings.

The glory of Portugal in India and in China
has departed. Her flag is now rarely seen in her
few remaining ports; her languishing trade is

carried on in foreign ships; the best houses in Macao are occupied by foreign merchants; her very existence in China is now upheld and supported by the commerce she was formerly so anxious to suppress.

Our settlement of Hong-Kong will withdraw the greater portion of that countenance; and Macao, if the great merchants leave it, will cease to be a place of importance.   From us they deserve no compassion; — we who have always regarded them with kindness as subjects of our ancient ally, and who have always offered them our powerful protection in the hour of need, have met with in return contumely, falsehood, and broken faith.   Macao is a true shoot from the old stem.

Saturday, 4th of June. — We took our departure a little before noon (the gallant Hoogly not being one of the fastest) to ensure our return to Hong-Kong by sunset.   By visits to China ware stores and repositories of curiosities our purses were more than sufficiently lightened.   The first cursory glance at the former disappointed me; with the exception of a few large bowls and garden seats, the shop displayed nothing but flaunting patterns, upon indifferent china, visibly made to order for foreign exportation.   But when the crafty old proprietor saw that we pertinaciously grasped some few samples of old Nankin porcelain which we had ferreted out from behind a pile of trumpery, and refused with great contempt even to look at his gaudy collection, he reluctantly produced specimens worthy of his country's reputation.

Immediately upon our arrival at Hong-Kong, I accompanied Keppel on board the Blenheim, where we found the Plenipotentiary and Lord Saltoun at dinner. Keppel received orders to sail with his convoy at daylight next morning. The Major-General in the Belleisle, and Sir Henry Pottinger by steam, take their departure two or three days after; so we may expect instant work.

As day broke on the 5th, the gun was fired and signal hoisted by the senior officer, and repeated by us, for the convoy to weigh. Eleven ships spread, or rather ought to have spread, their topsails to the breeze: however, they did so sooner than I expected, and we were on our way with the whole of them by 7 o'clock, attended by H. M. brig Serpent.

At first the monsoon was fresh and steady, until, on the afternoon of the fourth day, the wind chopped round against us, accompanied by thick rain, which has lasted to the present day, the 13th of June. We anchored off the Kwesan

Islands the night of the 11th.   Yesterday we made our number to H. M. S. Endymion, Capt. the Hon. Frederick Grey.   He left Hong-Kong a week before us, but had been detained by contrary winds and the dull sailing of some of his transports.   He was waiting for two stray ships.

All the afternoon of yesterday the weather was so thick we could scarcely see 300 yards before us.   A light air blew in fitful puffs from the North, and the tide ran strong against us.   The atmosphere was still and oppressive, and nothing was heard but the sound of the heavy surf on the distant beach and the strokes of the ropes against the masts, as the ship rolled to the seaward swell. In such weather duty is a labour, and the tired officer of the watch was looking with a wistful eye at the steam rising from the good things on the table of his mess below, when his attention was aroused by a booming sound from the N. W., resembling the irregular fire of heavy artillery. It came from the direction of Chusan, where a mere handful of men was left to garrison the large fortified town of Ting Hai, full of inveterate and vindictive enemies.   At intervals throughout the afternoon, until nightfall, we fancied that the same sound was repeated.

To-day the remainder of our convoy arrived led by the indefatigable little Serpent.   The thick bank of mist rose for a period, and the fleet tripped anchors. We anchored again in the evening, the fog as thick as ever. On the 14th the weather cleared, and we weighed with the tide and wind both in our favour. The frigate led the van, while the Dido whipped up the rear under topsails. We passed Buffaloe's Nose on our left, and traversed a winding channel between high verdant islands, cultivated to their summits. Embankments faced with stone were thrown across every shallow inlet to collect the alluvial deposit for paddy-fields, and up the slopes rising from these there were a number of neat villages and farm-houses, shaded by fruit trees and surrounded by their little compounds. The only vestige of timber I saw were a few firs and groves of bamboos lining the narrow watercourses. We observed labourers in the fields, who hardly ceased their work to gaze upon us, nor did the fishermen in the boats we passed evince either fear or curiosity. Every object to us was full of interest, and I fear I may be in consequence induced to commit the unpardonable sin of prolixity.

We left the southern shore of Chusan on our right; saw a large French frigate at anchor at Spithead, the name that has been given to the outer roadstead, and anchored off " Just in the

way," a small islet in about the centre of the
North-Western Channel, and fronting the harbour
of Ting-Hai,—distance ten miles. Captain Grey
took the Vixen steamer in to get letters, orders,
and gain intelligence. In two hours he returned,
and the commanding officers of the troops and
masters of transports repaired on board the Endymion to learn their final destination.

During the interim a heavy thunder-storm
accompanied with squalls sprung up, and two of
the transports' boats drifted to leeward of their
ships, and would have been driven on shore, if
one of ours had not rendered them timely assistance. They were close to the reef when she
reached them, without anchors or arms, and the
crews completely exhausted. The night had set
in, and they could distinctly hear the people
speaking on shore. The Chinese had seen the
perilous position of our countrymen before it was
dark, and doubtless anticipated their capture.
However, our cutter's cable proved good, and the
three boats rode by it until the tide slackened,—
the loss of supper their only distress.

The steamer brought me letters from some
friends in the fleet. They write in high spirits:
they speak of the small but gallant force, and of
the glorious spirit of enterprise which unites both
arms of the service. They mention their onward

movement to Woo-sung, at the entrance of the
Yang-tze-kiang, a place which is said to be
strongly fortified; that is, after the Chinese
fashion, with their flanks uncovered and rear
open.

The next day we weighed with eight ships;
the Endymion with the remainder entered the
harbour of Ting-hai. The islands on our right
were beautiful; the little bays, receding in graceful curves, were full of junks; villages round
their shores nestling in bright foliage, and terraced
fields rising above them, interspersed with numerous lanes and hedge-row trees.

We passed Chin-hai to our left, and saw two
men-of-war at anchor behind the island. The
Union Jack waved from the fort that crowned
its summit.

We anchored for the night. The next day
we sailed between thousands of nets fastened to
stakes driven in six and seven fathoms' water.
As we almost rubbed our sides against them, we
could see their bags full of fine fish.

At noon we were within five-and-forty miles
of Woo-sung, with a fresh and favourable breeze,
and fair expectation of seeing the admiral before
nightfall, and fully anticipated being in time for
the coming event, when all our hopes were dis-
pelled by the distinctly heard sound of heavy

ordnance from the north-west.   Our anxiety now
increased beyond endurance, and although it could
not make the ship sail faster, it stuck her on the
ground, and as in duty bound, some of our convoy
kept us in countenance.   The tide, however, was
on the rise, so we soon floated and pushed on up
the river.

At five P. M. we saw the admiral's flag conspicuous above the masts of the smaller men-of-
war around it.   The transports and store-ships
were riding in the offing, and the occasional
explosion of a magazine was the only evidence of
the recent destruction.

CHAP. III.

DISMANTLING OF THE WOO-SUNG FORTS. — CHINESE GAL-
LANTRY. — CONDUCT OF THE PEASANTRY. — SIR HUGH
GOUGH. — CHINESE CANNON AND THEIR INSCRIPTIONS.
TOWN OF POUSHUNG — ADVANCE INLAND. — TAKING OF
CHAN-HAI. — CHINESE TEA-GARDENS. — DWARFING PRO-
CESS. — PAWNBROKING DEPOSITORIES. — COMMUNICATION
FROM ELIPOO. — VISITS TO THE ARSENAL AND OTHER
PUBLIC BUILDINGS. — DISAFFECTION OF THE POPULATION
TOWARDS THE MANDARINS. — EXPLORATION OF THE
RIVER WOO-SUNG.

16*th June.* — WHEN we anchored, a pursy good-
natured officer came on board bursting with news,
which we were as eager to receive as he to
detail.

The night before the shallow and winding
channel was buoyed by Commanders Kellett and
Collinson, but not without being perceived by the
Chinese, who were so confident of their power to
repel us, that when they were under their strongest battery they gave three derisive cheers, but
did not fire a shot.

This morning the sloops Columbine, Clio, and
Modeste, and the well-known Blonde, were towed
into position by steamers, and the admiral followed

in his line-of-battle ship, where, in fact, many would have thought it imprudent for a frigate to venture.

The Chinese opened the ball, and with more spirit and skill than they had hitherto evinced. A brisk fire was maintained on both sides for two hours and a half. At one battery, after the embrasures were in ruins and almost every gun dismounted, a Chinese stood upon the ramparts waving a flag in the midst of the Blonde's magnificent fire.

Many instances of personal bravery have lately been observed, particularly among the mandarins. At Chapoo one fine old officer gallantly led his men twice to the very points of our bayonets, manfully rallying them after each repulse, until he fell shot through the loins. When he was carried to the rear, an interpreter, seeing tears streaming down his cheeks, told him not to fear — that mercy and every kindness would be shown him — " Mercy," he said, " I want no mercy. I came here to fight for my Emperor, and neither to give nor to accept mercy; but if you wish to gain my gratitude, and can be generous, write to my revered sovereign, and say I fell in the front, fighting to the last."

We repaired on board the flag-ship, and found the admiral in high feather, while half his officers were in a state of happy oblivion, trumpeting in longitudinal postures, in their cabins and upon lockers, after their day's fatigue.

The forts of Woo-sung guarded the entrance of the river of the same name. The mud ramparts topped the sea-wall, which is built to protect the vast alluvial plains from the inundations of the river. They do not exceed the height from the water of a line-of-battle ship's main-deck guns. They flank every winding turn of the narrow channel, and could be made, in the hands of experienced engineers, works as formidable as those of Cronstadt.

The river conducts to Chan-hai, and I have little doubt to the lake of Tai-hou, and consequently is the channel of communication through this province of Kieng-su from the two great emporiums, the cities of Sou-tchou-foo and Hou-tchou-foo.

On the 17th I attended the admiral on a tour of inspection round the eastern battery and a short distance inland. This was the side furthest from the shipping, and consequently the least damaged, but still the crown fort on the point, cased round with piles, and with two and a half feet of mud and stones jammed between, was riddled like a sieve, and the guard-rooms and small magazine in the centre smothered in ruins.

Broken gingalls, dismounted and spiked guns, arrows, spears, matchlocks, shot, and loose powder, besides hats and other articles of dress, were strewed about in every direction. The carriages of the guns were generally of the rudest description, but there were a few new ones upon an improved principle. The gun was fastened on a bed which traversed upon a fixed pivot in the centre of the carriage; the breech supported, when trained either to the right or to the left, upon a stool.

At first the peasantry kept aloof; but when we sat down to luncheon they approached without fear, at the same time intimating that the soldiers had all run away, and that they had no connection with them. We returned on board, leaving them peacefully occupied in their ordinary pursuits.

The next day I landed on the other shore, and accompanied the General-in-Chief on a tour of inspection. He had quartered troops along the lines, and in the two towns at their extremes, — Poushung, facing the Yang-tze-kiang, and Woosung, at an angle formed by a stream running due west from the river Woo-sung, comprising at least five miles of fortified lines. These the General intended to inspect on foot; all say, who know him best, that few young officers in his army can support what he frequently endures.

It must be remembered that a march of ten
miles with the thermometer 88° in the shade, and
the air dense and oppressive from recent humidity,
is not the light exercise that a ramble of twenty
miles over our own heathy hills would be to a
sportsman.   I remarked, however, that, although
so prodigal of his own strength, he was anxiously
careful of that of the soldiers.   Every sentry we
passed was directed to keep in the shade, and
cautioned if found unnecessarily exposing himself to the sun.

The scattered fragments of the recent work
were here much more considerable than on the
eastern side; several of the embrasures were literally knocked into one large gap.   Parties from
the ships were employed embarking the brass
guns, some of which were of great length, and
had more metal in them than European cannon
of the same calibre; but as they are cast muzzle
downwards, the feculence necessarily accumulates
at the breech, where the strength is most required;
so that I apprehend the risk is greater to the
gunner than to the foe.   They adopt the custom
common among many Eastern nations of naming
their guns.   Some of these were stamped with
Chinese characters signifying " The robber's
judgment," " The tamer and subduer of Barbarians; " and one tremendous fellow, upwards of

twelve feet long, was designated by the single title of " Barbarian."

The sea-wall, along which we walked, is a solid structure of wrought granite, with a brick, and occasionally a mud, parapet. We passed several dead bodies, and a wounded man, who had managed to drag himself to the edge of a canal. A grape shot had struck him above the knee and passed out at his hip; the poor fellow, forgetting we were enemies, implored our aid (a fruitless request in his condition to one of his own countrymen). He was carried to a station, and every attention shown him.

The town of Poushung is a square in shape, with streets running at right angles; those emanating from the centre front the four gates of the surrounding wall. The houses are mean hovels of wood; some of the large *Jos* temples are striking, but built of the same material to the roofs, which are handsomely ornamented with glazed tiles of different colours. The habitations were entirely deserted; and those we gained access to presented nothing sufficiently tempting to induce the plunderer to run the risk of flagellation.

On our return we met Mr. Gutzlaff the interpreter, who told the General he had received undoubted intelligence that the people of Chan-hai were actively employed removing their valuables, and that we should, he feared, be a day too late to secure a ransom.

We passed the smouldering ashes of a line of tents, and to our horror saw the roasting remains of their former occupants, probably some of the wounded unable to escape from the rapid conflagration. We visited the town of Wo-sung, embarked, and returned on board the Cornwallis.

It was arranged by the Commanders-in-Chief that the force destined to advance upon the city should be divided ; one half, including seamen and marines, to proceed by water ; the other, under the command of Colonel Montgomery, by land. I determined to accompany the latter.

On the 19th, at four o' clock in the morning, I landed on the banks of the rivulet before mentioned, just as the 18th Royal Irish were in the act of crossing. The 49th, Madras Native Riflemen, Horse and Foot Artillery, and Sappers and Miners, composed our force. The sky was clear, and the air full of that delightful fragrance peculiar to early morning, and the men were in high spirits in anticipation of an inland march, — rather a novelty to them of late.

We were *en route* by six o'clock, and an imposing sight these 2000 hardy fellows marching in single files along the narrow path-ways must have offered to the gaping Celestials. The country, flat as Kent and Essex by the banks of the Thames, is completely cultivated, and as beautiful as its sameness of features will allow fertility to make it. The flattened tops of earthen dykes between the fields are the only roads, and these are flanked, and here and there crossed by deep ditches, which we passed on granite slabs, generally too narrow for the Horse Artillery. This provoking but not unforeseen hindrance caused some trouble and much delay, the Sappers having frequently to fill the ditches for the passage of the guns. We trod drier ground as we receded from the river; and, besides the perpetual rice, saw fields of beans, corn, cotton, and other plants. Farms, surrounded by high shrub hedges, neatly interlaced with platted bamboo, were thickly scattered over the country. Nothing could be more rural than the appearance of the houses, some in clusters, others by themselves, all half hid by umbrageous inclosures, delightful lanes of fruit-trees, and abundance of wild honeysuckle and roses. Affluence and industry were every where apparent, and a love of neatness conspicuous from the arrangement of the house to the tilling of the ground.

We saw crowds of peasantry in every direction; they climbed the trees and little knolls to obtain a good view of us from a distance; but when a long survey convinced them that we were not

" frantically" disposed, they approached with confidence. Our handful of men would not have been a mouthful a-piece to the multitudes around us.

We passed two wounded men lying on a bank dying without assistance in sight of thousands. Unfortunately we could not afford them aid, advancing as we were through a hostile country.

We went through two villages; the shops were open, and the people remained in them; the first time such confidence had been shown towards us in China. Strict orders were issued to touch nothing, and to the credit of the thirsty troops be it spoken, they were obeyed. Almost every house has its little garden shaded by trees; among them I remarked the tulip, the tallow, and the mulberry. We flushed a pheasant or two, and I heard some partridges, during our march. The former bird is very plentiful throughout all Central China; at Chusan the officers in winter quarters had excellent sport.

Graves were in every field — mounds of earth, some hollowed into vaults, others solid with the coffin resting on the top, and covered with matting.

There appeared to be a great paucity of quadrupeds, although I venture to say every man in our little army kept as sharp a look out for beasts of the field and of the sty as for the enemy; as the wherewithal for dinner, to the best of our belief, still enjoyed the breath of Heaven. Two raffish ponies and a water buffalo were the only animals we saw.

At last, after a march of eleven miles, we approached a river, and had to skirt its banks for some distance to the westward, when we came to a bridge of five piers — single slabs of granite spanning a space of twenty feet at least from the shore to the first pier. These were flapped over by others of the same length to the second, and so on to the last, the upper slabs being in the centre. When we had crossed the bridge, we were in the suburbs of Chan-hai. The way to the city gates inclined to the left ; the shops along it were partially shut, and the people in a state of great excitement, sometimes coming in our line of march with basins of samstchu, which they offered to the men as an irresistible bribe, and for which they got well drubbed ; but the greater proportion clustered together in stupid terror round the tea-shops, and at the entrances of the narrow streets. Merchants' stores, warehouses, builders' yards, and what I took to be distilleries, indicated our approach to a large and wealthy city.

A soldier of the advanced guard fell back to inform us that we were close to the walls — formed in close order, the advanced guard fell back,

and on we went double quick to the closed gates.
We saw through a crevice two small guns pointed
to sweep the causeway, but not a sound was
heard. We scaled the wall by an old house, ap-
propriately placed; found the ramparts deserted,
and saw the townspeople flying. The gates were
opened; the bugles struck up; and the troops
marched through.

After taking formal possession, we proceeded
along the ramparts to a *Jos* house, erected on a
bastion, and commanding a view of the river.
We saw our steamers coming up with the North
Star, Modeste, and Columbine in tow. When
within two miles of us, a small battery, which we
had unavoidably passed far to our left, opened
fire upon them. It was silenced in five minutes.

The appearance of the town, considering its
rank as a second " chop " city, disappointed me.
Certainly the shops were shut and the streets
deserted, but yet the houses were generally
shabby and insignificant, built of wood, the upper
stories projecting over the narrow streets.

The General took up his quarters in a pavilion
built on the edge of a sheet of water in the public
gardens of the Ching-hwang-mian. To convey
an adequate notion of these shall be my endeavour,
as they are so completely Chinese in taste, idea,
and execution.

In the centre of a serpentine sheet of water, there is a rocky island, and on it a large temple of two stories, fitted up for the accommodation of the wealthy public. Pillars of carved wood support the roof; fretted groups of uncouth figures fill up the narrow spaces; while moveable latticed blinds screen the occupants from the warmth of the noonday sun. Nothing can surpass the beauty and truth to nature of the most minutely carved flowers and insects prodigally scattered over every screen and cornice. This is the central and largest temple. A number of other light aerial-looking structures of the same form are perched upon the corners of artificial rocky precipices, and upon odd little islands. Light and fanciful wooden bridges connect most of these islands, and are thrown across the arms of the serpentine water, so that each sequestered spot can be visited in turn. At a certain passage of the sun, the main temple is shaded in front by a rocky eminence, the large masses of which are connected with great art and propriety of taste, but in shape and adjustment most studiously grotesque. Trees and flowers and tufts of grass are sown and planted, where art must have been taxed to the utmost to procure them lodgment.

In another part of the gardens there is a miniature wood of dwarf trees, with a dell and water-

fall; the leaves, fruit, and blossoms of the trees
are in proportion to their size. This ingenious
science (if science it can be called), to bring it to
perfection, requires the most assiduous care and
patient watching.* A small branch of a forest
tree is deprived of a ring of bark, and the bare
place covered round with prepared unctuous
earth; this is kept moist, and when the radicals
have pushed into the loam, the branch is separated
from the tree, and planted in a trough or porcelain
flower-pot. The pot is then filled with bog earth
manure and clay, and water is applied according
to the necessity of the plant. The branches are
repressed by cutting and burning, and bent into
shapes resembling an old forest tree; and even
to the roughness of the bark and hollow knots of
pruned and decayed branches, they are complete
in resemblance. The roughness is produced by
ants, attracted by smearing the bark with sweet
substances.

Tortuous pathways lead to the top of the artificial mountain, each turning formed with studied
art to surprise and charm, by offering at every
point fresh views and objects. Flowers and
creepers sprout out from crevices; trees hang over
the jutting crags; small pavilions crested with

* Davis's China, p. 331.

the white stork, their emblem of purity, are seen from almost every vista, while grottos and rocky recesses, shady bowers and labyrinths, are placed to entrap the unwary, each with an appropriate motto, one inviting the wanderer to repose, another offering quiet and seclusion to the contemplative philosopher.

Three regiments were quartered in these gardens, and the rooms formed for the enjoyments of the wealthiest were occupied by the private soldier, and many of the most exquisite ornaments were torn down and burnt to cook their numerous messes.   Nor could this be well avoided : they had just entered quarters after a long march; no wood was at hand, and there was no time to send parties to search for it, and fuel it was of course necessary the men should have.   Round these fires the soldiers might be seen sitting enveloped in silk and satin cloaks lined with rich furs, exciting a blaze with embroidered fans, lawful property taken from the Chinese caught with these pilfered articles about them.   Such *loot* was easily obtained in a large Chinese town, owing to the general practice of placing things in pawn. These depositories are numerous, always well stocked, and consequently the first places to be broken into by the rabble preparatory to our

D

assaults, and after the respectable inhabitants had left the town.

The first thing that strikes one upon entering a captured city is Chinese robbers, passing, like a string of busy ants, in a continuous line, from some large house to the city gates, heavily laden. In this pursuit the Fokiens are the bravest of the brave. They will bear thumping, kicking, and maltreating in every way, but will most pertinaciously hold to their bundles.

I quartered upon my kind friend Colonel Montgomery and the artillery. Their *locale* was a pawnbroker's house; the lower rooms and courts, which we occupied, were spacious and empty, but the upper suite of apartments was filled with shelves and stands laden with rich stuffs. A smaller room, set apart for the reception of gold and silver ornaments, had been partially ransacked of its contents. Broomsticks were in requisition to clear our future premises of the rabble, but not before the goods of greatest value had been abstracted.

The Coolies proved themselves of keener sight than their masters, by the capitally supplied board we sat down to, — principally the result of the day's forage.

When the merry laugh and hearty tone of good fellowship were changed by my tired companions to a nasal trumpet note, I endeavoured to excite a proper feeling of romantic enthusiasm worthy my novel position; — under a Chinaman's roof, in a city of a central province of the Celestial Empire, honoured for the first time by the presence of English masters; — but it was of no avail; pagodas and mandarins, ships and soldiers, feasting and fighting, images of dead and dying, and, lastly, happy peaceful England, flitted past my drowsy vision, until the comforter of the wretched, and friend of the weary — sleep, overpowered me.

The next morning I sallied out to see the town, and call upon the General-in-chief. He was in conference with the Admiral about a letter which a well-known character, designated by the appellation of Corporal White, had brought from Elepoo. This petty mandarin (Corporal White) was first known to the expedition when up the gulf of Petchelee, off the Pei-ho. He was then the medium of communication between Admiral Elliot and Keshen.

We examined numerous *Jos* houses, some covering a greater extent of ground than Westminster Abbey. None possessed beauty of architectural design ; all were elaborately ornamented, and contained rows of gilded wooden deities of the *Budha* faith, three times the size of life.

We visited a public hospital under the charge of some priests of Budha; the wards, surrounding an enclosed court, were full of spectres dying from disease and recent neglect. The medical staff did all that humane and clever men could do to alleviate their sufferings, but they had neither time nor remedies at hand to amend their condition.

Hence we went to the Arsenal, where we found ten pieces of flying artillery mounted on wheelbarrows. In fact, the carriage was precisely like a large garden barrow, with a locker before for the shot, and a drawer between the handles containing loose powder and a small shovel to load with. Besides iron guns of various calibre, we discovered some new brass 12-pound carronades, modelled from one lying by their side, having on it the crown and "G. R. 1826." With the difference of the crown, in the place of which there was a Chinese character, they were exact copies. Close to them was a new circular slide for a Paixhan gun; probably the design was made from drawings taken by some of the Chinese occasionally detained on board our steamers.

This is not the first instance of their talent and expertness as copyists, and satisfies me that this war will do them (in some respects) more good than harm, by sharpening their wits, and will render a second, at any future period, a much more difficult undertaking.

Upon the approach of our fleet to Woo-sung, the Chinese governor issued notices assuring the people that our final destruction was at hand — that they might rest in confident security, and prepare festivities to welcome the glorious day on which the "barbarian eyes" taken in the battle would be sacrificed. Shortly before our arrival, it appears that the mandarins had nearly "squeezed" all the patience out of their long-enduring inferiors, and that in consequence the sufferers had the audacity to complain of oppression. Our onward movement naturally alarmed their masters, and produced these proclamations. The consequence was, that after the forts of Woo-sung fell, the people retaliated, and denounced the mandarins as traitors and cowards for running away on the first approach of danger, and vowed they would never permit them to return. My informant was Mr. Gutzlaff, who seemed to consider this unusual independence of sentiment a favourable omen.

We have reason to believe, from information collected since our arrival, that the Woo-sung is the principal river of communication to the central country, through which the great canal passes, and into, by various branches, its largest reservoir, the lake of Tai-hou; that instead of the coasting produce passing directly up the Yang-tze-kiang to the canal for distribution through the empire, the portion destined for the inland provinces to the southward is transported by this tributary. This belief was further confirmed by an examination of an old map by a French Jesuit, procured by Major Anstruther, and which he had most ingeniously and satisfactorily compared with a Chinese book of maps found in our quarters.

21st of June. — I was one of those who accompanied the Admiral up the Woo-sung in the Nemesis. We were attended by two other steamers with 400 marines on board. From Chan-hai the river leads in a southerly direction for twenty miles, retaining the same breadth (which is equal to the Thames off Gravesend) and extraordinary depth of from six to eight fathoms. Passed two large streams on our right leading to the towns of Sing-kong and Song-king. Their position is marked by two pagodas of seven stories, conspicuous above the trees. As it wound to the S. W., distance thirty miles from the town, we passed some forts destroyed the day before by Captain Boucher. Opposite these, another large river entering from the eastward (the name of which we could not ascertain from our pressed informants) communicates with the town of Sing-te, which is situated on its banks; thirty-three miles, estimated distance, the river swept round from the N. W., with a depth of water sufficient to float a three-decker; forty-five miles, the river divided into two great streams, one extending towards the N. W., the other to the northward. Three Chinese we took from separate junks agreed that the northern is the right one to take to enter the lake, and that it is deeper than the other; both of which assertions I am inclined to doubt. As we proceeded, armlets became numerous entering our main stream in every direction through low swampy ground. Unfortunately we could not ascertain our latitude by the sun's altitude.

We embarked on board the Medusa, a flat-bottomed iron steamer, and pushed up the river, now scarcely double the vessel's breadth. After proceeding two miles we became convinced that we had entered a subordinate channel, which was soon proved, by information obtained from a hardy, intelligent-looking boatman we caught for the purpose. We retraced our steps out of this creek, and for about three miles down the continuation of this delta of armlets, when he pointed out a branch to the N. N. E., which he positively asserted led into a great lake; so we conjectured that we had mistaken the main branch, which probably enters the lake at its eastern extremity,

and had passed into a minor river that must run
along a portion of the N. E. shore, and is drained
by the low swampy ground of the greater part of
its waters.

Unfortunately the Admiral could not afford
time, or we might have extended our research up
the N. W. artery, which, if it leads to the lake
(and there can be little doubt of it), places at our
mercy Sou-tchou-foo, the richest manufacturing
city in the empire after Canton, and round which
we know coal and iron of excellent quality
abounds.   We boarded three junks laden with
the former most useful article.

The country retained its level surface as far as
we went; the same alluvial soil throughout; the
whole apparently under cultivation of rice, the
staple produce of the southern half of China.
The only relief the eye experienced from the
sameness of prospect were three conical hills,
rising abruptly from the plain to the height of
about 400 feet.   As these were in a parallel latitude with the division of the river, we were at one
time inclined to think the lake washed their
base; but our upward course proved this conjec-
ture extremely improbable.   It strikes me that
the whole of this great flat was originally the bed
of the estuary of the Yang-tze-kiang, and that
these islands of the plain may be the apices of

hard strata remaining prominent after the loose parts had been washed to a level.

The weather was, unfortunately, extremely unfavourable. It rained in torrents the greater part of the day, and a lowering vapour obscured the distant prospect. The population appeared to be as dense here as elsewhere. Numbers of men and some few children approached with great confidence and more curiosity than I had hitherto observed them evince. During the rain, those working in the fields wore large capes of leaves fastened together like thatch, and hats made of the same material, with a rim as broad as an umbrella.

I boarded a punt with Captain Troubridge; it contained a woman and two men, beside being laden with bundles of rice-grass ready for re-planting.* They seemed very glad to see us, and appeared much amused at my companion showing them how to plant rice, uttering " Iah ah!" after each bundle as it was flung into an adjoining swamp until they were all expended, when their countenances elongated considerably. We thought we had been doing them a favour:

---

* They pull up and replant their rice after it has attained a certain growth.

unfortunately, it was not the place designed for the reception of their crop.

At 4 A. M. we were again at anchor off Chan-hai, and embarked the troops before eight o'clock to return down the river to the shipping. The same day we were at anchor off Woo-sung.

CHAP. IV.

OBSERVATIONS. — THE YANG-TZE-KIANG. — ISLAND OF
SUNG-MING.

ALL our reinforcements have arrived: 73 sail are
now at anchor around us; the surveyors are forty
or fifty miles to the westward buoying the passage; and we only wait their return to proceed
up the Yang-tze-kiang to Nanking, the old
capital of the Chinese empire.

I believe it is thought by some in England
that time is wasted while the operations of the
expedition are confined to the southward, and
that the final blow must be struck at Pekin,
against which city we ought in the first instance
to have proceeded. But, in considering the
chances of success of the mode of operations that
has been adopted, it should be remembered that
the capital rose from being an obscure village in
a comparatively unfruitful country to its present
vast size and opulence only through the fostering
care of an arbitrary government, and aided by
the advantage of its being chosen for the seat of
the Imperial residence; the crowds which flocked

D 6

to it in consequence were soon more numerous
than the entire population of Petchelee besides.
The capital thus became necessarily dependent on
distant sources for its support, and the great
canal was cut to convey the absolute necessaries
of life from the southern provinces to its numerous
inhabitants.

Such being the position of the capital, it is
certainly reasonable to hope that all the practical
objects of the war will be most quickly attained,
and that an equally impressive moral effect will
be produced, by selecting that course of action in
which we are now engaged, rather than by
making a more direct attempt on Pekin.

By striking into the heart of China by the
Yang-tze-Kiang through Keang-soo, Gan-hwuy,
and even to Ho-nan — with Nanking in our
hands, the Woo-sung and, above all, the Imperial canal under our control; having Sou-
chou-foo, with its riches, its iron and its coal
dependent on us, by our possession of Chap-pu
and Chan-hai, and with the power our position
on the great lines of water communication will
give us over the important branches of national
industry, the manufacture of silk at Hang-
tchou-foo, and the porcelain trade, of which
King-te-tching is the emporium — we shall
effectually have Pekin at our mercy. The go-

vernment cannot then continue any prolonged resistance to our just demands, without incurring
the risk of disaffection through all its territories,
caused by such an interruption to trade and
industry, while it will be still more coerced by
the immediate inconvenience to which all classes
in the capital will be subjected by the deprivation
of the means of subsistence.

I therefore anticipate that such a mode of
making war will prove much more effectual than
would a barren conquest of Pekin, deserted as we
should probably find it by the court and the
wealthier classes.

All geographical surveys of China are necessarily very imperfect, as is exemplified by the
great inaccuracies as to the coast line upon the
maps of our most eminent geographers, Wyld and
Arrowsmith, both of whom, I presume, have de-
rived the greater portion of their information from
maps made by the Jesuits. It is in the position
of places that they are mostly incorrect, but the
general features of the country, towns, ranges of
mountains, the source and size of rivers, and
extent of plains, seem, as far as our observations
have extended, wonderfully accurate.

The Yang-tze-kiang, one of the finest and
most navigable rivers in the world, strictly
speaking, takes its rise from the northern moun-

tains of Upper Thibet, traversing a course
through that country and China Proper of 3237
miles.   It runs to the southward through Thibet
under the name of Petchou; through a small
portion of Sze-chuen under that of Muh-loo-soo
and of Kinsha ("golden sanded"); through the
remaining portion, as also in its course through
Yun-nan, and where it again traverses parts of
Sze-chuen to the northward, which are inhabited
by the tribe of Meaou-tsze; thence it takes the
name of Yang-tze-Kiang at the distance of
2800 miles from the sea, which length is given
in consequence by many authorities as that of the
whole river.   It flows through Thibet, Sze-chuen,
Hoo-pih, a portion of Keang-se, Gan-hwuy, and
Keang-see to the ocean.

This noble river is supposed to be navigable to
the borders of the empire.   It is broad, deep, and
sometimes very rapid; islands rise from its extensive bed, and are amongst the most fertile and
densely populated portions of the empire.   Numerous tributary streams are fed by its floods, and
these are connected by canals forming a network
of water communication.

Our present anchorage off Woo-sung is opposite
the great alluvial island of Sung-ming, said to
have risen above the water since the thirteenth

century, and now containing a population of nearly two millions.

At this season of the year all the grain and treasure are transported by the canal to the northern provinces ; so our chiefs are most anxious to establish a blockade of that main artery as soon as possible, and the viceroy of Kiang-see, being well aware of our intention, is, they say, using every exertion to get these all-important supplies across the river before our arrival.

" So let's away ;
Advantage feeds him fat while men delay."

CHAP. V.

SURVEYORS' RETURN. — SAILING OF THE FLEET. — DE-
STRUCTION OF A FORT. — PAGODA OF TONG-SHOU. — CHI-
NESE PROCLAMATION. — DESTRUCTION OF THE SE-SHAN
FORTS.—CAPTURE OF A FUGITIVE.—ASCENT TO A PAGODA
BY MOONLIGHT. — CHINESE FISHING TACKLE.

THE 5th of July was a day of eager excitement.
The steamers that had been absent with Captains
Kellett and Collinson (our two active surveyors)
had returned with the gratifying intelligence that
the channel, although in some parts intricate and
narrow, was very deep and sufficiently clear for
the largest ships to traverse.

The signal was made to prepare for sea for the
following day, and the order of sailing was issued
by the Admiral.

The army was divided into four brigades under
the command of Major-Generals Lord Saltoun,
Berkeley, Schoedde, and Brigadier Montgomery
of the Artillery. These were distributed in five
divisions, each division led and under the entire
charge of a man-of-war: Captains Boucher of
the Blonde, Hon. F. Grey of Endymion, Hon. H.
Keppel, Dido, Kingcome, Belleisle, and Kuper,

Calliope, were the officers appointed by the Admiral.

It is not easy to describe the feeling of exultation which more or less animated all at the prospect of entering as invaders into the heart of an immense empire, where we are looked upon as " barbarians from beyond the civilised world."

The Admiral weighed on the 6th, at day-light, with a fair wind, the first and fourth divisions following. The General-in-chief at the head of the first, Lord Saltoun in the Belleisle, Captain Kingcome leading the fourth. A distance of two miles separated each division. We in Dido were last — a most tantalizing position.

Grey's division passed at noon, when the wind grew very light, and the tide began to ebb before our turn arrived to weigh ; so we found we could hardly stem it. The headmost ships were by this time out of sight, when we, scarcely a league from our former berth, were obliged to anchor ; the Blonde, in charge of the second division, on shore, six miles ahead ; one of Captain Grey's and one of our own convoy in the same condition : heavy rain commenced ; the light air entirely abated, and we became most anxious.

7th of July. — The wind was fresh and foul, but the weather very fine ; the dark thick vapoury clouds had rolled way, and a clear, bright, dry, blue, speckled sky, with knotty dappled clouds high up, appeared.

Keppel gave me his gig to pull up to the Admiral. On my way, eight miles from the Dido, I boarded the Columbine; she had just anchored off a creek supposed to communicate with the river Woo-sung, which poor despairing Morshead was ordered to blockade. He was very sorry for himself, and could not bear to look at the ships passing. However, all cannot win lottery prizes, and withal it was of the utmost importance that the outlet should be guarded. I condoled with and really felt for him, and after devouring a great portion of a Chinese ham, in which he could not keep me company, I shoved off and stretched over towards Sung-ming, and ran along its shore until the tide changed, when I bore up for the H. C. S. Auckland at anchor in the centre of the stream.

Mr. Lay the interpreter was on board, acting the part of a good commissary for the benefit of the combined forces. When I arrived the ship was surrounded by junks, each containing from two to three water buffaloes, besides pigs and baskets of poultry. It was difficult to determine which were the noisiest, the pigs or their masters.

The natives of the island had been compelled by threats to give up about eighty buffaloes — a forced but not an unjust exaction, as they received in payment from eight to ten dollars per head, besides the benefit of our future protection. At the same time I have no doubt that this necessary demand on our part caused them a temporary inconvenience, as, from the evident marks of the yoke the animals bore, they must have been used for agricultural purposes.

At half past eight P. M. the tide slackened, and I proceeded up the river in my boat. I plainly saw the Cornwallis at sunset at anchor about seven miles ahead off Harvey Point — the western extremity of the island, named after poor Harvey, a midshipman of Captain Bethune's ship the Conway. He was killed two years before, while employed upon a survey.

A sharp pull placed me by eleven o'clock on the flag-ship's quarter-deck, much to the surprise of the officer of the watch, who for some time was at a loss to account for my nocturnal appearance.

8th of July. — I was up early, and found the Admiral already on deck ; he welcomed me most kindly. Weighed with a fair breeze at seven o'clock, all the divisions in sight coming up in famous style. Under the pilotage of Captain Kellet we ran up five-and-twenty miles without a stoppage, generally keeping the northern shore on board. Where the river shoaled much towards the centre, or where the course was winding and irregular, the surveyors had moored Chinese sanpans for beacons. Some of these had been swept away by the stream, or cut adrift; but they knew the various bearings, and we passed on without detention or mishap.

The country continues a low and level flat, with occasional exceptions, at long intervals, of a few cone-shaped hills, jutting up without the prelude of undulating ground or change of feature. We anchored opposite one of these, on the south bank close to the shore, and sent an armed party under the command of the first lieutenant, accompanied by Mr. Gutzlaff, to destroy a small fort even with the water and backed by the rising ground. The garrison of the fort absconded before our men entered, leaving behind them a few old iron guns, besides some brass ones of more modern construction. The former were destroyed and the latter shipped.

We saw between the trees the ancient and picturesque pagoda of the third-class city of Tong-shou; the town itself lies in a hollow surrounded by some fine old timber; the dilapidated tower marks its site from the river view.

9th of July. — We weighed about one P. M., the channel irregular and difficult, but had the satisfaction of seeing our magnificent line of ships wind through in safety. It must have been a grand, and to use a Chinese term, " awe-inspiring " sight to the dense crowds everywhere lining the banks — this gallant fleet stretching along their fertile shores as far as the eye could reach, their light upper sails reflecting the bright sun over the tops of the tallest trees, and threading their way past dangers for the first time without a stoppage, sometimes within a stone's throw of the shore, at others in the centre of the stream, where the current runs the strongest.

This struck them with astonishment. At the commencement of the floods (the present period) they do not think the upward passage in their largest junks practicable ; so generally transfer their cargoes to smaller vessels, able from their lesser draught to skirt the shore and take advantage of the eddies.

10th of July. — We remained at anchor the greater portion of the day, waiting the return of our indefatigable pilot-fish, the two small steamers. In the evening we weighed, and ran on till sunset.

11th of July. — We were under all sail before breakfast. After a few miles ascent the south shore varied from the hitherto tame unchanging prospect to a diversity of abrupt hills. On the summit of one which we passed we observed a square

tower with a peaked roof, resembling much our
copies from those of the Flemings. I fancy it
must be intended for a watch-tower, a structure
in common use; but as far as my observation
has extended, this stands single in originality.

In a valley behind the hill we saw a pagoda of
seven stories; opposite to it on the northern bank
are two remarkable hillocks, on which there are
towers. These we named the Pagoda Hills. They
offer excellent landmarks to assist the navigation
of the river. We passed them rapidly, and anchored in the evening.

The river here is five miles broad at least, the
channel from nine to twelve fathoms deep, in
some spots even upwards of twenty fathoms.
The country continues verdant and abundantly
populous; creeks and canals numerous, that
have their entrances concealed by water-flags,
which bind miles of shore, and protect the
embankments from the rush of the passing
current.

12th. — Weighed in the forenoon, and with the
wind N. E. ran up a portion of the river. Our
calculation, made from our uncertain chart, placed
us only fifteen miles from the great canal; the
information gleaned from the peasantry, forty
miles.

13th. — The current here is much more rapid,

still varying slightly at the periods of rise and
fall of tide; but even at the slowest, rolling onwards four miles an hour.

The river has narrowed to about 4000 feet;
the reaches are also shorter, and in one or two
spots, the spits and shoals off the convex shore jut
out with steep sides into the deep water, sometimes
shoaling in a ship's breadth from seven fathoms to
a few feet.

Two small steamers were always kept about
four points upon the bows of the flag-ship, and the
Modeste, Captain Watson, half a mile a-head, to
lead the way and signalise the soundings.   She
upon one occasion shoaled her water in about
her own length, from, I think, eight fathoms to
fifteen feet, and had to throw all aback to save
herself (which she did in admirable style), dropping a buoy to mark the spot as she again made
sail.

The steamers are up the river surveying, so we
remain at anchor.   Sent boats on shore for vegetables.   They found the people very friendly;
willing to supply our few wants, and anxious to
show every civility.   Sanpans came off with some
fish caught in suspension-nets, seen at almost
every league along the river's banks.   They
averaged about six pounds in weight, were something of the shape of the salmon, but had yellow

tails, and were covered with larger scales than our northern fish.

The party returned on board loaded with supplies. They had read a proclamation stuck against the principal house of the village. It mentioned our victories, and hinted at the possibility of our ascent up their great river; in the event of which occurring, the people were implored to remain in their houses, and not to leave the country exposed to the inroads of banditti; it stated that we (the English) had always shown ourselves anxious to conciliate the peasantry, and consequently would not injure them, nor allow the robbers to commit depredations, if they remained. This single document is of itself, I think, evidence sufficient to lead to the conclusion that the Emperor will never again have the inclination to command, allowing he may have the power to compel, his subjects to retire inland, and thus meet an invading enemy by passive resistance. It would expose his richest provinces to be plundered by native robbers, — the evil, above all others, he has the greatest reason to dread.

On the 14th the steamers returned. They had seen the pagoda of Chin-kiang-foo, the wealthy city and Tartar stronghold, situated off the south mouth of the great canal. They had been fired at from a fort upon the hill of Se-shan, a high and bold eminence, which we could just see seven miles before us.

Weighed at nine, A. M., and with a commanding breeze stemmed the current rapidly; the water deep, the river wide, and the scenery rich and smiling.

The winding of the river kept the approach to Se-shan from being very apparent for some time; but when we rounded the last elbow, we saw it in full view descending precipitously into the river.

The Admiral summoned us to an early dinner, to be in readiness for work by the time it was finished.   At four o'clock we were close to the hill, which in shape is rather peculiar.   It rises abruptly 400 feet from the plain on one side, and from the river on the other, sloping to a valley which divides its centre.   At the bottom, and on the face of this hollow, two batteries were erected; a partial fire commenced from each of these upon the steamers and leading sloops.   The Modeste was ordered to commence action, which she no sooner did than away the garrison scampered, throwing their uniforms off as the ascent up the hill grew pressing, their movements occasionally accelerated by a few 32-pounders making ricochets after them.

I landed with the storming party sent to take possession, blow up the powder, disable the guns, and destroy the forts.   We found a great deal of

E

loose powder lying about covered by temporary
sheds and in boxes half buried at the rear of the
batteries, besides shot, gingals, matchlocks, bows
and arrows, and other munitions of war. In the
houses we found some hot messes of rice and
vegetables, and several ponies, which the soldiers
had left in their haste to effect their escape.

Leaving the work of destruction to proceed, I
ascended a narrow ridge leading to the top of the
hill, — a desperate fag, considering the great heat,
and one I had not anticipated while looking up at
the winding path from below; but the extensive
prospect seen from the summit spread out around
would have amply repaid me a much greater exertion. Inland, towards the S. E., this detached
cluster of hills broke into undulating country
clothed with verdure, and fir plantations bordered
small lakes confined in natural basins. Extending
my view beyond, I saw the windings of the
vast river we had ascended; our ships were still
scattered over its broad surface, the sternmost
divisions of the fleet coming up under all sail. To
the other side I turned with yet greater interest;
there the land in the foreground continued a low
and swampy flat, leaving it difficult at a little
distance to determine which of the several broad
waters, winding in serpentine channels through the
country, was the main branch. I looked down

upon innumerable square sheets of water, separated from each other by narrow mounds of earth; they covered the surface of what we knew to be arable land, but which more closely resembled a vast lake, intersected by many causeways. Willow trees grew along their sides, and here and there small patches, somewhat higher than the common surface, supported cottages and farm sheds. Beyond this again, towards the west, the pagoda of Chinkiang-foo was observable; it is built on a slight eminence eight or ten miles in advance, by the river's course, from where I stood. The sun had set some time; the mists rose from the marshes, until it became the only object in the distant view.

I was not alone. Lieut. James Fitzjames had gained the summit before me, and I found him, when I arrived, sitting upon a granite rock, quite out of breath after his ascent. His coxswain, who had followed him at a slower pace, descried a martial hero under a bush, whom he captured and dragged up by his pig-tail. I verily believe the poor wretch thought we were going to eat him, which supposition said little for his estimation of our good taste. Had he been a firm, sleek, clean, and portly gentleman, it would have been another thing; but this was a poor devil

E 2

whose flesh had left the bones from the constant use of opium.

Our further admiration of the prospect was interrupted by an explosion: the barracks and houses were all on fire, and our party in the boats waving to us to return; so we had to descend at a pace which did not suit our companion the prisoner, who fell upon his back and resigned himself to despair. Fortunately the descent was steep, although perhaps somewhat rough; so down he went in a sitting posture between Fitzjames and his coxswain, and reached the bottom in safety; but, I shrewdly suspect, with the loss of more than a tailor could replace.

15th of July. — We remained at anchor all day, waiting for the surveying officers, who were up the river. We heard the sound of cannon; the steamers returned in the evening, and informed us that they had been fired upon from a masked battery placed to guard the passage, between the island of Seung-shan and the S.W. shore. The Phlegethon silenced their fire without loss on her part, and dismounted some guns; but did not destroy them, as it was contrary to the Admiral's orders to land.

16th. — The wind, which had from the commencement of our ascent up to the present time blown steadily in our favour, changed during the

night to light variable airs; so that, within ten
miles of the imperial canal, we were doomed to be
tantalized by detention.   In the evening I went
on shore with Captain Watson for a walk; the
sun was setting when we landed, and the evening
was so cool and delightful that we determined to
visit a pagoda on the summit of a hill two miles
inland.   We passed round the base of Battery
Hill and through a prettily secluded village of
farm-houses, with their offices attached.   We
found the inhabitants sitting upon stools before
their doors, eating their evening meal of rice and
fish ; they received us with good humour and apparent confidence; — (not that they had great cause
to be afraid of two unarmed gentlemen in white
jackets, attended only by a guard of two men
with muskets, and with a peasant for a guide
whom we had pressed for the occasion.)

We commenced our ascent by moonlight; it
was a rough walk, but the exercise and freshness
of the night dew was a delightful change after
the heat of the day and our recent confinement.
Our path led across two valleys, over the breast
of a steep, and round the ridge of a stony crescent forming one side to a basin, at the foot of the
eminence upon which the pagoda stood.   As we
fagged up a flight of broken steps, hewn from the
solid rock, and of most penitential length, the

old grey tower fronted us in imposing grandeur, thrown out in prominent relief from the dark sky by the clear moonlight. The stillness of night, unbroken except by the sound of our own footsteps, might cause a superstitious imagination to endow it with vitality, and make it appear to swell in bulk and rock to and fro as the passing shadows of the flying clouds obscured its surface, like a huge giant menacing the approach of his pigmy disturbers. Then, in the eleventh hour, we began to think that our excursion was not the most prudent thing we could have undertaken; particularly as we remembered that the *Jos* houses attached to pagodas are frequently used for temporary barracks, and for the accommodation of public officers and their retinues when upon a journey. However, it was too late to recede, so we passed through the tower, which we found partly in ruins, to the *Jos* house at its other side, and knocked at the principal door. Some time elapsed before our summons was answered; at last we heard whispering, and then a demand of (I suppose) what we wanted, which our guide answered; but from fear that he would tell them who we really were, and thereby effectually prevent our entrance, we always stopped his mouth after he uttered the first syllable; trusting to Chinese curiosity for accomplishing the rest. We were not mistaken; after repeated questions, and of course most unsatisfactory replies, the door was opened, and to the great surprise and terror of the priests we walked in. The poor padres were all alone, and had been some time in bed before we made their acquaintance. They, however, had the hospitality to offer us a mess of rice and flour, simmering on a slow fire, and which they gave us to understand was constantly kept ready, day and night, for strangers and passers by.

From the elevated and isolated position of their hill, the view must be commanding; we of course could see but little through the hazy moonshine. We gave them two dollars and departed.

On the 17th light and variable puffs flew round the hill of Se-shan, and made it perfectly impossible for the fleet to weigh, as no ship could pass this rapid portion of the river without a steady breeze, owing to the bottom being very irregular, and the eddies in consequence numerous and strong. Captain Napier and I went on board the little steamer Medusa, generally denominated the Cornwallis's child, in consequence of her size and constant attendance upon the flag-ship. She was ordered to tow the Starling up to continue the survey; we accordingly weighed, but had not proceeded far when the latter vessel grounded,

and the day was lost in attempts to get her off.
During the interim we (Napier and myself) ex-
plored sundry creeks among the bulrushes, and
discovered some old trap-nets of peculiar construction : they were formed (round several strong
bamboo supports) of rushes growing from the
bottom, plaited into various recesses, with passages between each, and ending in a chamber,
like that of our stake-nets.   We also surprised a
fisherman and his boy sculling a punt; they were
using a horse-hair line made like ours, and with
hooks snooded at short distances baited with
winkles, the barb passing through holes drilled in
their shells for the purpose.

Our little vessel floated in the evening; a severe
day's work for the men in the sun, considering the
thermometer was 92° in the shade.

18th of July. — At 4 A. M. we weighed, and,
with the schooner lashed alongside, proceeded up
the river.   After we were freed, by the aid of
that precious vapour, steam, from the thraldom of
eddy winds and chow-chow water, the freshening
breeze from the old quarter induced us to cast off
and send the steamer back.   Being able, from our
light draught, to keep close to the shore, out of
the strength of the current, we made famous way,
and in a short time saw the island of " Seung-
shan," at the lower end of the straight reach into

which the south entrance of the imperial canal opens.

As we passed onwards, the features of the scenery to our left changed from the dead level to an undulating country, varied by a series of smooth surfaced hills, inclosing within their circuit plains and broad valleys. The greater portion of these hills was clothed with long rich grass, and had the appearance of being eminently adapted for pasture lands; but not a flock nor herd or single head of living animal could we see even with the aid of our glasses.

CHAP. VI.

THE island of Seung-shan occupies half the
width of the river, and, by obstructing the free
passage of the water, doubles the rate of current
passing its sides. In the channel to the left
great blows force themselves up from deep cavities,
followed by powerful whirlpools, formed from
the rush of water into the empty spaces. These
are sometimes of sufficient force to turn a frigate
moving under the power and weight of an eight-
knot breeze. The right-hand passage is broader,
and the current not so rapid; but then, again, the
navigable channel is narrower; and if the wind,
which frequently blows in puffs round the island,
lulls at the critical moment, the vessel will to a
certainty be swept upon a large flat shoal under
her lee.

We got through the rapid passage after four

attempts, — the Blonde, Modeste, and Childers
having all tried it in vain. Whirlpools caught them
when in the centre, whirled them round, and sent
them down the stream for some distance, as helpless as boys, toy-boats in a running brook.

Seung-shan, a rocky cone with a surface soil
which nurtures luxuriant groves of tropical vegetation, is, like its sister, Kin-shan, or " golden
island," imperial property. Priests are the only
occupants; temples and palaces the principal
buildings, surrounded by gardens and bowers.
As we passed it slowly, we had time to observe
the massive granite terraces, decorated with large
stone monsters, and having convenient and handsome flights of steps descending to the water; fine
temples placed to be seen, and yet shaded by
useful and ornamental plants; open pavilions and
secluded summer-houses embowered amidst the
bright arbutus, which was enlivened by red-
berries and paddy birds nestling amidst its foliage,
like bunches of white blossoms.

Opposite this little paradise a plain honest rock
of reddish granite, broken into an upright cliff,
descends precipitously into the river; in the
centre of its face a round hole is neatly excavated
with a slight step before it, and some Chinese
characters marked above it. While we were
conjecturing what this singular orifice could be

for, out came a figure dressed in a rusty brick-coloured gown, and made the ko-tow most obsequiously. We concluded him to be a recluse living upon charity,— a sort of Fuckeĕr,— common characters in the East, not less so in China than in India, but in this country a wiser sect, living a less purgatorial life than those of Hindostan.

Close to his abode, on the low land at the foot of the rocky promontory, we saw the remains of Phlegethon battery, and the smouldering ruins of the magazines. A party having been landed from the Blonde to destroy the dismounted guns, they found some brass pieces among the number, which, as prize property, were shipped. After traversing the narrow strait we entered the long reach between the two islands. Over the sloping brows of some low hills, across two valleys and a plain beyond, we traced the high and well-built wall of Chin-kiang-foo, with its square and round flanking bastions. High above a conspicuous gate, a red and yellow flag waved, but not a man was to be seen along the whole range of the extensive ramparts, nor in the suburbs, which extended to the river's edge. All appeared to us as deserted and lone as a city of the dead. Little did we then think that in a few days this large, powerful, and wealthy city would in reality be what we by chance compared it to.

The Blonde's masts (which ship had preceded us) were visible above the flat land forming the bend to the N. W., and close to the upper mouth of the canal; she was placed there to stop the traffic until the fleet could ascend. We continued to pass up at a rapid rate, and were soon abreast of the island Kin-shan, bedecked with gay and fantastic buildings. The tall golden-tipped pagoda, and ranges of imperial temples and palaces, roofed with yellow and green glazed porcelain tiles, glittered in the sun. It reminded me more of some of those fancy pictures of enchanted islands, than anything I had ever before seen. It is smaller than Seung-shan (or, as we have named it, " Silver Island "), and is a more perfect bijou of a place, although, after all, to our English eyes it has rather a toy-shop appearance.

When we closed the Blonde, Captain Boucher ordered the little Starling higher up to blockade a creek, supposed to bend round by the base of the ridge of mountains to the south, and communicate from thence with the canal below the city, and again into the river above where we lay. At the mouth of this creek we could not get bottom in the centre with twenty fathoms; so anchored in ten fathoms, almost among the rushes.

After dark a large fire broke out in the direction of the town. This set us completely on the alert,

as we thought it might arise from fire-rafts; but
that idea was soon altered by its stationary position, and we became aware that the suburbs of
the city extending to the water were in flames.
Shortly after a larger conflagration flared up to
windward, which we could distinctly see by the
glare that arose from a number of junks, and which
we afterwards ascertained had been fired by native
robbers.

Napier and I boarded two junks that were at
anchor just above us. They were two peaceful
traders, the one laden with rice, the other piled
up like a floating haystack with the reeds they
use for repairing the canal banks. They were, nevertheless, towed clear of our hawse, and we betook
ourselves to rest, which, however, was frequently
disturbed by the incessant attacks of the most
pertinacious mosquitoes I had ever seen or felt.
These for some time we vigorously encountered,
but at last we were vanquished by their per-
tinacity. In several instances, these disagreeable
little insects have proved a serious evil, the wounds
they inflicted having turned into bad sores upon
many of the men whose constitutions were probably affected by their salt diet.

19th of July.— I took up my quarters for a day
on board the Modeste; she was anchored on the
northern shore, across the mouth of the canal, and

upon my arrival was surrounded by punts full
of men and vegetables, fish, bullocks, and all the
good things the country afforded.   These were
intended as cum-shaw (presents) to bribe the
" illustrious eye" (as they designated Captain
Watson) to allow their private trade to continue ;
and I was much amused watching their faces of con-
temptuous astonishment when they were desired
to charge a price for every thing they brought,
as no presents of the sort would be received.

All respectably dressed persons were allowed to
come on board, and to wander about wherever they
pleased.   They seemed particularly struck with
the cleanliness of the ship and fittings of the
guns ; they were timid at first, but soon regained
their self-possession, and at last became so familiar
that they bored one, and had to be corrected
occasionally by a slight application inflicted by
the master-at-arms.

The Admiral arrived in the afternoon and
anchored off the town, much below where we
were lying.   In the evening we determined to
attempt a passage to his ship by an inland canal,
which Captain Watson thought communicated
with a creek entering the river opposite the
Cornwallis.

We pulled up in his gig past a temple of the
Dragon King, or genius of the water element, and

who, Mr. Davis says, is supposed to have the
canal in his special keeping. It is close to the
right-hand shore, and conveniently situated for
the crews of the passage boats to repair to, to
offer at the shrine of the idol propitiatory sacrifices
preparatory to crossing the river.

After we had pulled a mile we turned down
a branch to the right, and in sight of a bridge of
junks which Watson had constructed to block
up the canal above this entrance. We landed and
walked some distance along the banks; they were
skirted by willow trees, resembling those along
the borders of several of our canals in England.
Rows of old dwellings, densely inhabited, extended
behind them. Although the dress and features of
the people are the same as those we meet upon the
coast, the variations in construction and appearance of the houses, boats, the mode of propelling
them, and various other minute differences, are
very apparent. The roofs are straighter, and the
material burnt or baked brick instead of wood,
while there is a more respectable and aged cast
about the public buildings, which command a
certain reverence I never could feel for the gaudy
flaunting structures of Fo-kien and Quan-tong.

Little expecting to see the strangers in their
remote creek, none of the women had removed
either from the villages or junks, which they

had hitherto invariably done previous to our approach; not that I think such a proceeding was ever voluntary on their part, nor, in fact, is it in the nature of the charming sex to possess less curiosity in China than in Europe.   In the present case, however, though many fair dames rather put us out of countenance by their stedfast stare, others were really frightened ; and I sincerely pitied the poor creatures as they hobbled away on their small feet, and in their haste stumbling at every step.

God knows how this barbarous habit of cramping the feet first arose : whether from jealousy on the part of the husbands, or merely a freak of taste, which first became the fashion and then a universal custom, no satisfactory explanation has yet appeared, nor can the Chinese themselves clearly account for its origin.

Many Chinese reprobate the habit, but yet will not marry a woman with large feet, because the small ones are supposed to convey the idea of delicacy and gentility by rendering their poor owner unfit for labour ; and while they admit the process of dwarfing the foot to be cruel, all affirm that the result is a decided beauty.   I must confess that I began to think, with many others, that a Chinese lady would appear to want some peculiar grace without the deformity of the crippled feet, — so much does custom guide and regulate what is commonly called taste. How true it is that a fashion, however absurd in itself, when once generally adopted, must be followed by the most sedate and sapient, or they lose the semblance of wisdom and appear ridiculous. It is therefore not surprising that the Chinese consider us in the latter light, as all our habits, manners, forms, customs, appearances, and dress are so diametrically opposite to theirs.

Habit has so much influence over that inexplicable idea beauty, that many will concur in the assumption of Sir Joshua Reynolds, "that if we were more used to deformity than beauty, deformity would then lose the idea that is annexed to it, and take that of beauty."

Perhaps his theory would be more applicable if confined to the easy adaptation of a preposterous habit, without the assumption that habit will subvert the taste to an opposite extreme; because, I think few associations that were distasteful when first impressed upon the imagination could alter so materially, as subsequently to convey the exquisite sense of beauty. Custom may reconcile and suppress a disgust, but cannot exact a pleasurable sensation without adding some other agreeable attribute under the wing of which the original distaste may find cover and protection.

For instance, after years of absence in tropical

climes, where the bright sun is rarely obscured by
stationary clouds, and where exuberant verdure
presents beauties unknown elsewhere, and where
the very softness of nature is almost in itself a
charm sufficient to render life happy; we may approach the shores of Old England, and enter the
dense belt of atmosphere that sometimes surrounds
our country, and derive actual pleasure from the
first saturation received from a heavy fog; by it
the depths of memory are awakened, and the inconvenience is absorbed by the charm of the re-
membrance, which, while it lasts, will force all who
ever felt the power I speak of to acknowledge
that they would not exchange the inconvenience
for the bluest sky, — so intimately are our emotions connected with and governed through the
agency of our former sensibilities.

The means taken to effect the alteration of the
women's feet in China are decidedly prejudicial
to the health, and frequently attended with fatal
consequences.

This fact was ascertained by a clever young
naval surgeon who was for some time stationed
at Chusan. It happened that during an excursion
into the country, he one day entered a house where
he found a child about eight years old very ill,
and suffering under severe hectic fever; on examination he discovered that her feet were under-

going the process of distortion; he was informed
that she had been a year under this treatment.
Moved by pity for the little sufferer, he proceeded
to remove the bindings, and fomented the feet,
which were covered with ulcers and inflammation.
The change in shape had already commenced by
the depression of the toes. The child was much
relieved by, and evidently grateful for his treatment. On taking his leave he warned the mother
that she would certainly lose her child if the bands
were replaced; but his remonstrances were of no
avail. Whenever he returned (and this happened
frequently), he always found them on again, the
woman urging as an excuse that her daughter had
better die than remain unmarried, and that without improved feet such a calamity would be her
inevitable lot. As might be expected, the child grew
worse and worse. After a longer interval than
usual, he once again revisited the house, but found
it untenanted, and a little coffin lying at the door,
in which he discovered the body of his poor young
patient. Being a scientific man, he seized the opportunity of adding the feet to a collection already
commenced.

It is not customary to commence the treatment
necessary for the distortion of the feet until the
girl has reached the age of seven or eight; were
it begun sooner, it is believed that the feet

would be deprived by it of all vitality, and thus be lost entirely.   The operation generally requires from eighteen months to two years for its completion.   Of course the leg below the knee shrinks to the bone and loses all shape.

We walked along the banks for some distance until we came to the old wall of the ancient town of Kwa-chou, which we could distinctly trace running at right angles from the canal towards the north, until hid by a wild of rank shrubbery and old fruit trees, probably the neglected remains of the five famous gardens of Woo-yeun, many years ago the temporary residence of the Emperor Kien-loong. *

The wall had originally crossed the canal by means of an arch, for on both sides portions of it were entire, with rough extremities to the water's edge.

This is probably the canal mentioned by (I think) Lord Macartney, which was cut by the Emperor Kien-loong to secure a private route to Golden Island without having to pass by Kwa-chou.

We were obliged to get into the boat to pass the wall, and shortly after entered the suburbs of another village, going close by some *Jos* house

* Davis's Sketches in China, vol. ii. p. 2.

and under three bridges, each of a single arch, which were very fairly constructed; they were supported by wedged stones, but without a centre key-stone.

Many of the junks were full of children; I fancy, belonging principally to single families. In these boats, the lady, we could plainly perceive, monopolised the duties of captain of the vessel, as well as mistress of the household, even to the management of the sails and skulls. The little urchins all appeared happy, good-humoured, and old-fashioned.

As we advanced towards the river our view became circumscribed by the flags on either hand rising above the banks.

The country through which we this evening passed is pleasing and picturesque, —more so, indeed, than any I had hitherto seen; yet my walk did not convey the enjoyment, the pleasant satisfaction, that, after some slight confinement, one over a more indifferent country has frequently before excited in me.

Heaven knows I have no prejudice against this umbrella race; but, in regarding the Chinese, I can never get rid of the association of clock-work figures which are moved round their allotted surface by machinery.

China is a rich and fertile empire, and crowded with a most persevering and industrious people;

but it has not the splendour and romance of the
Indies, the noble energy and science of the north
of Europe, nor does it possess the refinement
nor the luxurious climate of the south of our
Continent, where the cold is modified by the intervention of mountains.

" Know'st thou the land where the lemon-trees bloom,
  Where the gold orange glows 'mid the deep thicket's
      gloom,
  Where a wind ever soft from the blue heaven blows,
  And the groves are of laurel, and myrtle, and rose ? "
                          GÖETHE'S *Wilhelm Meister*.

We found the notorious Corporal White * on
board the Cornwallis, charged with a message
and letters from Elipoo, who expressed himself
very anxious to meet our high authorities, to
ascertain what our demands were, and to enter
upon negotiations, which he affirmed he had
ample powers to do.   Sir Henry referred him to
his proclamation, which most fully explained all
he pretended ignorance of, and informed him that
when the necessary commission from the Emperor
was produced he would instantly receive the authorities intrusted with it.

On our way back to the Modeste we had to pass
close to " Golden Island ; " and as the moon was
up, we landed on a marble terrace, overgrown
with weeds.   It was no ordinary event to contem-

    * The mandarin before referred to.

plate a spot where no tradition told of western strangers' visit; where the brows of generations of priests had furrowed and withered, —their every thought, but those for their private interests, centred in their ruler and deity, the sovereign.

A terrace surrounds the W. and N. W. sides of the island, and extends along the front of two large temples, three pavilions, and the imperial palace, now in great decay. We knocked at the gate of the principal *Jos* house, and were admitted by a priest of Fo, who, to judge from his appearance, had just risen from his slumbers; his dull and sleepy eye, heavy frame, and lazy step, as he guided us through the building by the feeble glimmer of a candle, made from the tallow tree, denoted his inactive and unintellectual mode of life. The light he held partially revealed the huge gilded images, twenty and thirty feet in height, and of every form and shape that the fertile idolatry of Budhism has invented, ranged round the walls with their faces to the centre of the building, while the two grim war idols guarding the aisle of the principal entrance, identified the temple as imperial property.

We discovered this to be the church of a large monastery, controlled by a prior and brotherhood, who have charge of all the sacerdotal duties of the island, and are also responsible for the cleanliness and order of the walks and gardens. The back entrance is concealed from the front by an elaborately carved screen reaching to the roof, and supporting the image of their supreme deity. By this door we passed into a larged paved court, in which a handsome bronze vase or censer stood upon a marble base ; a flight of granite steps led from this court to a smaller temple containing a single shrine, and surrounded by private dwellings and cloisters.

The priest took us in succession over shrines and *Jos* houses, scattered up the face of the island to the top. They were connected by terraces decorated with flowers and shrubs. At last we descended by a wooded and serpentine pathway to the ruinous palace, and were shown the chair of ebony inlaid with mother-of-pearl (the only vestige of furniture remaining) in which Kienloong used to sit and enjoy the balmy breezes, " fanned by the happy spirits." The marble steps and slabs were dislodged and broken by intruding shrubs ; and the almost obliterated carving upon the decayed wood-work indicated neglect and the lapse of time since the departure of its last royal occupant.

The fairy palace and charming retreat of the morning, like youth's first aspirations, melted, as

F

many of those illusions do, upon the hard touch of cold reality.

The three pavilions at the angles of the palace and *Jos* house each contained a shĕ-pae, — the name of tablets erected by emperors to commemorate great events, or to honour the memory of illustrious men. These marble slabs, twelve feet in height and two in breadth, supported perpendicularly upon the backs of marble tortoises, and covered with inscriptions, recorded the visit of his Imperial Majesty, Kien-loong, and his present of them to the island.

This diminutive spot has been the temporary residence of two emperors and three empresses; but since the Manchow dynasty ascended the throne, the visits of the sovereigns to their fertile and more genial provinces of the centre and the south have ceased, with the above mentioned exception; so this, with other royal abodes, has been greatly neglected, and suffered to decay.

Early on the 20th, I went with Captain Watson up the river to destroy some fire rafts which we saw smoking to windward. They had all been fired too soon; a few had burnt even with the water's edge, and others we found aground on shoals close to the rushes. Junks that had been abandoned by their crews came floating down in great numbers, and were emptied as they passsed along, by bands of river robbers. Those at anchor, and in our track, we boarded, and turned the plunderers out, while Watson dispersed his squadron of boats to collect others at a greater distance, and conveyed them to a creek under the safe protection of our guns. Many were full of rice; each different quality separately stowed in hanging bins, which were fastened to the beams, and rested upon a platform above the kelson. The most precious grain was pressed firmly down, and the surface stamped in several places with the impression of a large seal, the mark of the owner, to guard against fraud or theft. Others were laden with oil, varnish, dried fish, samshu, oil-cake, dried sea-weed (like our dulse), sugar, lime, bales of common nankin cloth, besides wares and furniture of various description. Salt, a royal monopoly, we found in great abundance on board the largest and better finished junks: these appear to average about 100 tons burden, and are built in the shape of a crescent. They float upon the water like a willow leaf reversed, their high projecting sterns rising forty feet above the surface. They are built of pine, neatly put together and smoothly planed, and their sides are

F 2

covered with bright varnish, which the Chinese take great pride in keeping highly polished. The solitary mast of ninety feet and upwards, without a shroud or stay, steps in the centre, and is frequently a single spar.

CHAP. VII.

RECONNOISSANCE OF ENEMY'S POSITION. — SIEGE OF CHIN-
KIANG-FOO. — BLOWING IN OF THE GATE. — RALLY OF
TARTAR TROOPS INSIDE THE TOWN. — SUICIDE OF TOWNS-
PEOPLE. — CHINESE INTERPRETER. — WE EXPLORE THE
CITY. — RETURN ON BOARD. — UNIFORMS AND ARMS OF
TARTARS AND CHINESE.

AFTER we returned to the ship, I accompanied
the General to the top of the pagoda on " Golden
Island," to take a reconnoissance preparatory to
the morrow's landing. We had a fine commanding view of the whole country over which portions of our operations were likely to be carried
on. The undulating country to the southward
and westward of the city rises to a range of hills
seen running almost parallel with the river, until
intercepted and excluded from view by another
chain crossing its western extremity, and ter-
minating in a slope towards the N. E., thus
forming the entrance of an extensive valley.
Upon these latter heights we counted seventy-five
tents, pitched in two divisions, each division commanding an ascent, and within a mile and a half of
the S. W. angle of the city wall.

A great portion of Chin-kiang-foo was ex-

cluded from our view by a bluff upon the mainland opposite Golden Island. The suburbs over
the low ground to the west, and along the borders
of the canal for upwards of a mile, prettily
diversified by trees and gardens attached to the
houses, lay between the wall and us.

21st of July. — The morning of this eventful
day on which it was destined that the proud
spirit of the Chinese government should be
humbled by the total destruction of their most
important Tartar stronghold, dawned with unclouded serenity, and before the sun rose, the
General Commander-in-chief, his staff, and the
right brigade, had landed and occupied the bluff
hill, above mentioned, to the westward of the
city, from the summit of which we had, while
the remainder of the troops were forming, ample
time to contemplate the magnificent panoramic
view of the city on our left, and the ground and
heights to the southward, on which the encamped
enemy were drawn up in a line behind entrench-
ments. From an eminence, we saw that they
were in greater force than either our previous
reconnoissance or the information gained by the
interpreter led us to anticipate. Looking at
their extended line, I began to suspect that the
greater portion, if not the whole, of the garrison
had, during the night, joined the camp, anxious

to bear the brunt of our attack, and, by offering a stronger resistance without, perhaps save the city from injury. I, however, soon found this to be a mistaken supposition.

My kind friend, Sir Hugh Gough, allowed me to make myself useful as an extra aide-de-camp. I landed, and was with him throughout the day in that capacity.

It would be unnecessary in me to recapitulate the tactics and events of an action which has been recorded and read in every public paper; so I shall confine my description to the movements I saw occurring round the person of the Chief.

By the time the troops were all landed the sun was high, and its unclouded force was felt by many a poor fellow destined to succumb to its power.

The first brigade, under Lord Saltoun, began to move up the valley leading to the heights, followed by a portion of the artillery. The column of our men and guns presented a fine sight as they marched up the winding valley, at times partially hid, at times emerging from behind the slight acclivities connected with the heights where the Chinese were drawn up in line, cresting their strong position, their tents struck, and banners flying. The latter commenced a distant fire until the Bengal volunteers, sent to turn their right flank, charged them up the hill, when they gave way within twenty yards of our bayonets.

I accompanied the volunteers, and had an opportunity of remarking a peculiar feature in the character of the Chinese. We had to cross a paddy field and occupy a small village under a close and smart fire from the enemy. The village had not been deserted: some of the houses were closed, while the inhabitants of others were standing in the streets, staring at us in stupid wonder; and, although they were viewing a contest between foreigners and their fellow-countrymen, and in danger themselves, from their position, of being shot, were coolly employed eating their bowls of rice.

The sun was too hot for a race, and, as the Chinese ran well, I returned to the Commander-in-chief on a mandarin's horse which I had caught. I found the Admiral and the General sitting under the shade of some fine palms upon a hill, the top of which was crowned by several spacious buildings. They were waiting for the centre brigade to come up to storm the town.

Our position overlooked the city wall within fair gingal range. We plainly saw the Tartar soldiers on the ramparts, two or more to every embrasure and loop-hole, anxiously watching our

movements, and waiting for an onset to open fire,
which they soon did with spirit as we moved
along a high embankment level with the wall.
Along this we continued a considerable distance
until we reached the enclosed suburbs, through
which we passed in security to within a short
distance of the western gate, connected with our
side by a bridge over the canal in front of it.

A gun was sent forward, with an advance party,
to cover Captain Pears and his Sappers, while he
blew the gate open.   This gallant service was
performed in admirable style under a cross fire
from flanking bastions.   The heavy, massive gates,
bound and studded with iron and propped on the
inside by many sand bags, flew in like chips, carried before a sudden blast of wind, and were hurried
along the street to a considerable distance, but
without one stone or brick of the gateway arch
being displaced, the calculation was so admirable.

Our gallant fellows dashed through with a
cheer in the midst of smoke, dust, and flying rafters.
Their impetuous charge would have driven back
five times their number, but no such opposition
was met with: we found instead, the ramparts in
the possession, at one point, of General Schoedde;
at another, of our seamen and marines, under the
command of Captain Peter Richards, who had
landed to recover some boats and guns disabled in

their ascent up the canal by an unexpected and destructive fire from an angle of the wall : at this angle Captain Richards escaladed and repaid the former loss with interest.

It was about mid-day when the centre brigade joined the left upon the ramparts. Soldiers were dropping at every step from exhaustion and excessive heat, so the General ordered a halt for a few hours, where we then were, round the west gate guard-house, merely sending a large detachment along the ramparts to the right to occupy the southern gate. This party had not proceeded half a mile when they encountered a sharp and sudden resistance from a large body of Tartars, drawn up on an open space before some houses, and flanked by a hedge, a ditch, and pond of water. They planted their gingals before them; formed with order and steadiness, and commenced a rapid and well directed fire, which brought down officers and men in quick succession. Our men, though taken somewhat by surprise, and not one to three, fired a volley and charged down the bank, driving all before them, but not without obstinate resistance.

As the enemy retreated through the compounds and narrow streets, our men were called off; a guard placed over the dead and wounded, and the rest sent forward to their destination.

The firing brought the General up, who re-
solved, when the sun became less powerful, to
sweep the town from house to house.

As we marched along the walls I saw, what as
a novice in this description of warfare shocked me
much, old men, women, and children, cutting
each other's throats, and drowning themselves by
the dozen ; and no one either attempting or apparently showing any inclination to save the poor
wretches, nor in fact regarding them with more
notice than they would a dead horse carried through
the streets of London to the kennel.

While we were resting in the south guard-house,
a Chinese Canton interpreter, who had frequently
before been the medium of communication between
the authorities of both nations, was introduced
under the escort of two soldiers : he was the
bearer of letters to our chief from the Viceroy :
they were to the old purport, requesting them to
send the ships down the river, and arrange a meeting with him on shore to settle differences.   Such
a modest request at such a time was exceedingly
mal-à-propos, and very nearly cost the stupid old
interpreter his life; who, fancying himself secure
in his knowledge of our language, passed through
the gate, and was nearly shot by the sentinel for
advancing towards the General's quarters, after
having failed in his endeavours to make himself

understood. Sir Hugh was in no humour to receive him, which he, having lost but little of his self-confidence, thought exceedingly incorrect. He said that " Elipoo wished very much to have a talkey outside river — no inside — and that English very bad if they no obey."

Our reply was, (I mean that given by our individual selves, who had nothing to do with the matter,) that " Englishman may talkey a very, very leettle, if Chinamen pay 20,000,000, and afterwards pay more, talkey more," and then the respectable old gentleman was shown the way out.

Towards evening an advance was sounded, and the Commander-in-chief marched with two regiments towards the Tartar quarter of the town, guided by some Chinese and Mr. Gutzlaff. We broke into many houses where we imagined soldiers were concealed, but met with no resistance, nor saw any armed Tartars. Quiet and peace seemed to reign paramount in the still evening, while the fragrance of the flowers surrounding almost every house calmed the strong excitement that had possessed us throughout the day. It was the prettiest Chinese town I had seen : the houses were all well kept, and the interiors of many magnificent; the streets well paved and clean; and open grassy spaces and gardens gave a grace and airiness not usually met with in walled cities.

We were guided to a large building said to be
the governor's palace. We saw that it belonged to
government by the flying dragon painted upon the
wall opposite the great entrance ; but the gates
had apparently been closed for some considerable
time : weeds were growing before them, and the
only sign of life was a wounded Tartar of great
size and strength lying under the shade of the
portico ; he was dressed in the blue over shirt
with yellow trimmings, said to be the uniform of
the imperial guard. When we forced the house
we found it equally deserted, but completely furnished, and of great extent. We set fire to it and
marched on.

I went with two soldiers of the 18th down
a street to the right, to a large house, which I
concluded belonged to a Tartar of consequence :
we burst the door and entered. Never shall I
forget the sight of misery that there met our view.

After we had forced our way over piles of
furniture, placed to barricade the door, we entered
an open court strewed with rich stuffs and covered
with clotted blood ; and upon the steps leading to
the " hall of ancestors " there were two bodies of
youthful Tartars, cold and stiff, much alike, apparently brothers. Having gained the threshold
of their abode, they had died where they had
fallen, from the loss of blood. Stepping over

these bodies, we entered the hall, and met, face to face, three women seated, a mother and two daughters; and at their feet lay two bodies of elderly men, with their throats cut from ear to ear, their senseless heads resting upon the feet of their relations. To the right were two young girls, beautiful and delicate, crouching over, and endeavouring to conceal, a living soldier.

In the heat of action, when the blood is up and the struggle is for life between man and man, the anguish of the wounded, and the sight of misery and pain, is unheeded; humanity is partially obscured by danger; but when excitement subsides with victory, and the individual circumstances are recalled to mind which led to the result, a heart would be hardly human that could feel unaffected by the retrospection. But the hardest heart of the oldest man who ever lived a life of rapine and slaughter could not have gazed on this scene of woe unmoved.

I stopped, horror-struck at what I saw. I must have betrayed my feelings by my countenance, as I stood spell-bound to the spot. The expression of cold unutterable despair depicted on the mother's face changed to the violent workings of scorn and hate, which at last burst forth in a paroxysm of invective, afterwards in floods of tears, which apparently, if any thing could,

relieved her. She came close to me, and seized
me by the arm, and with clenched teeth and
deadly frown pointed to the bodies — to her
daughters — to her yet splendid house, and to
herself; then stepped back a pace, and with firmly
closed hands, and in a hoarse and husky voice, I
could see by her gestures spoke of her misery —
of her hate, and, I doubt not, of revenge. It was
a scene that one could not bear long ; consolation
was useless ; expostulation from me vain. I attempted by signs to explain, offered her my
services, but was spurned. I endeavoured to
make her comprehend that, however great her
present misery, it might be in her unprotected
state a hundred-fold increased ; that if she would
place herself under my guidance, I would pass
her through the city gates in safety into the open
country, where, doubtless, she would meet many
of the fugitives ; but the poor woman would not
listen to me ; the whole family were by this time
in loud lamentation ; so all that remained for me
to do was to prevent the soldiers bayoneting the
man who, since our entrance, had attempted to
escape.

I left them, to return to the Commander-in-
chief.

As apparently all the soldiers had either
escaped, or thrown off their uniforms, and mixed

unknown with the crowds of townspeople, further search was useless.   The evening was waning
apace, and quarters were yet unprovided; fas-
tidiousness and the difficulty of choice between
the many spacious houses were the only obstacles
likely to delay a speedy arrangement; at length,
these *important* embarrassments were removed by
the discovery of a treasury, in a part of a very
extensive public building surrounded by a wall,
and enclosing a colonnade sufficiently large to
quarter several regiments.

Stiff and weary, and without a change of clothes,
I determined, as there was no occasion for my
staying, to return to the ship with Mr. Gough, a
son of the General, who happened to be in the
same plight with myself. With a small guard
we marched along the ramparts for a mile to the
western gate. The moon was up, and shone with
clear and tranquil light upon the silent town,
lying like an amphitheatre at our feet; so still,
so smiling in the placid beauty of the scene and
hour, in sad mockery of the misery and despair
of its concealed and wretched inhabitants. From
the gate we took charge of a wounded officer to
the boat, and by ten o'clock I was on board the
Cornwallis.

Throughout the day both the Chinese and
Tartar troops evinced a determined bravery,

which commanded our respect; and I believe I may safely say, that the upper classes, from the first to the last, have shown by their conduct that they cannot brook defeat; for, although we have captured many a Mandarin, we were never able to keep them prisoners for any length of time, they having either starved themselves by refusing to eat food, or otherwise committed suicide.

The Chinese have shown many individual instances of conspicuous gallantry : it may be sufficient to remark one in particular that occurred on the ramparts of Chin-kiang-foo. A Mandarin led a small party of about thirty men against a company of General Schoedde's advancing column; a volley dispersed his soldiers, but he marched up to the points of the bayonets; and, after firing his matchlock, succeeded in pulling over the ramparts with him two of the grenadiers.

I feel persuaded that, if drilled under English officers, they would prove equal, if not superior, to the Sepoys; they have greater physical power, greater obstinacy, and, consequently, minds that retain impressions with greater tenacity, and would be slow to lose confidence after it was once built upon the foundation of their vanity.

Their favourite arms are the gingal, matchlock, and bow and arrow; besides these, they have the spear, a halbert resembling that formerly used by our sergeants, a battle-axe, and an instrument not unlike a hedge chopper, fastened on a long pole; also the sword, both double and single handed.

A gingal resembles our wall-piece, and some carry a two-pound ball: it is supported upon a tripod, and requires three men to work and carry it, and is a very serviceable weapon.

The matchlock-man carries the charges for his piece in bamboo tubes, contained in a cotton belt fastened round his waist. He loads without a ramrod by striking the butt against the ground after inserting the ball; the consequence is, that he can charge and fire faster than one of us with a common musket.

When they fire from walls or entrenched camps, the best marksmen are stationed in front, and supplied with matchlocks by people whose only duty it is to load them.

The barrel of a matchlock is about the length of a Greek rifle, and is generally very accurate. If we had had a less active General, our loss during the war would have been very considerable; as it was, the Chinese had but little time given them for ball practice.

Their bows possess little strength, and are not equal to the arrows, which are strong and well made.

Besides these arms, they have rockets, and also

arrow-rockets, which I believe I may safely say did no harm throughout the war.

The dress of the Tartar and Chinese soldier is the same, only distinguished by the colour of the trimming. The common uniform consists of a quilted shirt, hanging down outside to the hips; an iron head-piece, and long boots, covering the thighs, made of cotton or satin, and with thick soles. At the commencement of the war, many of the troops used chain-armour; latterly it was discontinued.

CHAP. VIII.

DURING the forenoon of the 22d, the boats of
the fleet were employed landing provisions and
baggage for the brigade ordered to remain behind.
I went on shore with Captain Grey to walk over
the scene of the " last day's slaughter." Inside
the city we could hardly pass along the streets
for plunder; crates of beautiful China, bronze
ornaments, vases, satins, silks, crape, and gold
embroidery; besides, bales of meaner articles
were strewed about in every direction. The best
had been selected and carried for a short distance
until a new object attracted the pilferer's eye,
when the old was cast away and trodden under
foot. The Chinese were the most numerous and
systematic plunderers.

The work of death was still progressing.
Captain Grey and I entered a house, where we

saw twenty bodies of women and young girls, some hanging, others extended upon the floor ; all had either committed suicide, or been destroyed by their relatives. A panic had seized the unfortunate inhabitants, and every second house contained self-immolated victims. We saved several lives, but they were to the destroyed as drops are to the ocean.

On our progress to the General's quarters, we lost our way by leaving the ramparts, and entered a portion of the Chinese town hitherto unvisited. Apparitions from the lower regions could not have caused greater consternation among the crowds of unfortunate people, busily collecting their goods, and sending their wives and families into the country by a postern gate that had escaped our notice, than we three (including a middy of the Endymion) produced among them, particularly among the poor women, many of whom, I fancy, had seldom, if ever before, left the precincts of their gardens. Some were very good-looking, and all had a grace peculiarly their own. Two poor creatures, evidently belonging to the higher class, had blackened their faces to conceal their beauty—a thin disguise to the prying eyes of licentiousness. However, it is my belief that less villany was perpetrated than could have been reasonably expected, taking into consideration the anarchy that always for a time prevails in a captured city. Those they had cause to fear most were, beyond all doubt, their own countrymen.

The absence of all birds and beasts of prey struck me as being a strong evidence of the denseness of the population, and of the highly cultivated condition of the country. If there had been many in the country, or within hundreds of miles of us, their natural instinct would long ago have drawn them to the proximity of our camp.

Upon our arrival at the Commmander-in-chief's we found the prize agents packing up the treasure, which, however, proved inconsiderable — not more than 60,000 dollars worth of Sycee silver. In the same room with the silver they discovered a quantity of opium in small portions, hermetically enclosed in wax, each separate piece about the size of a roulette ball, and stamped and numbered, so precious do they consider this dangerous drug.

On the 24th, at about 5 A.M., I landed with the Admiral at the base of the bluff brow below the city. We met Sir Hugh Gough upon the hill, who was there to meet us. He took us round the summit to show a small cast-iron pagoda, which Gutzlaff told me is, from the inscription and characters, marking the epoch by their form, at least 1200 years old : that would carry its origin back to the *Tâng* dynasty.

It stands between thirty and forty feet high, at the base about eight feet in diameter, and is filled in with bricks to the summit.   Each of the seven stories is a separate cast: groups of figures ornament every side of the octagon ; and it is easy to be seen were cast in good relief, although now much time-worn.

Anxious to know something of the use or traditionary history of this singular tower, I went with an interpreter into the adjoining *Jos* house to demand an explanation from a priest, who we found had just risen from his mosquito curtained bed.   But whether our sudden appearance had terrified him, or whether from want of practice he had lost the use of speech, I cannot affirm, but to all my questions the silly old man did nothing but grin and laugh until the tears ran down his cheeks.

The emotion of fear must produce a different sensation in a Chinese from what it does in other people, for, when most afraid, they invariably laugh the heartiest ; rather against the theory of Mr. Hobbes, that " the passion of laughter is nothing else but sudden glory arising from some sudden conception of some eminency in ourselves by comparison with the infirmity of others, or with our own formerly."

This height would be a fine military post, and is to be occupied by Major-General Schoedde's brigade while we are up the river. It not only commands the town in a military point of view, but an agreeable and extensive prospect, and is by far the most airy spot that could be chosen.

On our way back to the ship we destroyed a water snake about seven feet in length. They abound in these waters; but I have not heard that their bite is so fatal as that of those which are met with amongst the islands of the Eastern Archipelago.

25th July. — Landed with the Admiral before 5 A.M. Ascended the hill, whence the General reconnoitred the enemy the morning of the attack. As I looked upon the fields and numerous roads of communication to and from the city, I observed strings of Chinese crowding every way, as busy and systematic as ants, going empty handed and returning laden. As well as I could see, they carried their loads some distance into the country, and were relieved by accomplices, who, I imagine, had small boats in waiting among the rushes, a considerable distance from any creek.

Another immense gang — almost an army — was gradually surrounding a great public building, plainly with the intention of committing open burglary.   The Admiral saw this, and questioned a countryman, who said it was a depository of some government monopoly.   General Schoedde, who happened to be near, was informed of this, and he quickly sent some artillery to disperse the rascals.

26th. — Major Malcolm came to the Cornwallis by times this morning, to entice me up the river to inspect about three hundred junks, for the purpose of selecting two or three from among them to carry ponies.   They were collected up a branch, or rather partition of the river, under charge of the Blonde.   After breakfast we went to the Blonde, and got a boat from her to the junks. These vessels look very cumbersome, but are admirably adapted for the canals and rivers they have to navigate.   Their draught is light, capacity for stowage great, accommodation above the deck excellent, besides their high sterns giving the facility of overlooking the tall rushes every where bordering the river and creeks of the low country.

We boarded numbers, some in shape almost a crescent, others more like a shoe, while many were straighter in their sheer, and sufficiently spacious to carry two troops of cavalry ; but these were too large and clumsy for our small detachment. We also felt some commiseration for the owners of the flax, hemp, rice, sugar, &c., they were laden with, much of which it would have been necessary to discharge, to render them available for our purpose.

We sent our boat back for the men to get their dinners, trusting to the pilotage of a Chinaman nearly blind from ophthalmia, and who with his sanpan we pressed into service. Under his guidance we went a mile higher up, and fortunately found among the last batch two craft of the required dimensions, the one empty above the deck, on which were built the cabins, and well ballasted with oil jars. The sliding panels unshipped, and left a clear space into which we afterwards introduced ten horses. The other was a smaller vessel, somewhat larger than a line-of-battle ship's launch, and apparently built for conveying passengers. The two cabins and galley occupied the entire upper space, only leaving a sufficiency of room before all, for the capstan. Instead of panellings, light open trellised screens, beautifully carved and polished, surrounded the vessel, admitting a free circulation of air; and if the weather happened to be cold or stormy, these could be closed by shutters made of pearl oyster shells *, sufficiently clear to admit the light.

* They have little or no glass in China.

The cabin was upwards of six feet high, and the deck in hatches was dry-rubbed, as also the furniture, to a polish that would have done credit to a cabinet maker.

We had not the heart to turn this little vessel into a stable, so she eventually became our yacht. We kept the captain and crew on board to work her; they received a stipend and their food, and proved good and zealous servants.

These Chinese are curious people. They evinced little or no surprise at our appearance; submitted with the greatest apathy to our unceremonious examination, and although by ourselves in a native punt, obeyed our orders to weigh without a question.

Two days after the action, while viewing the ruins of the Tartar General's house — his funeral pile — where, like a Roman of old, he sat himself down in his spacious hall, when all was lost, and desired his faithful attendants to obey his last command — to complete their last service by firing the building — Mr. Morrison discovered a man hid among the bushes in the garden: he proved to be the civil secretary of the late General, and had letters and papers about him of consequence. He was carried off as a prize, with the budget to be examined and translated on board the Queen. He spoke of his lost master with great feeling, and described him as one of the best and noblest of men.

Some of the despatches were from him to the Emperor, others from the Sovereign. The former gave a faithful account of our movements from Woosung to the day of our anchoring off Chin-kiang-foo. He expressed his unalterable fidelity and determination to fight to the last, but at the same time conjured his master, with the prophetic foresight of a doomed man, to end this war, at least, until their warlike resources were more systematically arranged, and the troops recruited and concentrated. He alluded to our science and energy, but did not allow that the barbarian's Queen possessed more devoted, or braver subjects than his august master. He mentioned all his own arrangements and readiness to await the attack, and, if joined by some expected reinforcements, his expectations of success. He concluded by saying, that his walls were high and in good repair, and that the city, which some years before beat back an organised banditti amounting to 300,000 men, might be able to repulse a few " barbarians."

The Emperor's letters are full of reproaches for battles lost, accusations of cowardice against men who had died bravely while he was writing these bitter letters, and threats in the event of future failure.

About this time, Sir Henry received a letter
from Ke-ying, who introduces himself as " an
unworthy connection of the imperial house," and
who mentions that he had journeyed from the
north to see and to hear realities and truths.
" Why should they not," he wrote, " meet to
speak, and mutually endeavour to level the mountains of separation and unite the gaps of discord,
before they widened to a gulf, over which there
would be no passing ? "

The letter itself is a beautiful appeal to the
feelings of humanity — an eloquent remonstrance,
cleverly omitting all mention of the points at issue.

In consequence of Ke-ying's reputed worth and
illustrious birth, Sir Henry Pottinger thought it
right to answer his letter officially. Mutually
with him he regretted the war, its cause and long
continuance. Driven at last, after great forbearance, to avenge insulted honour, nothing could
stay our indignation but ample redress, an acknow-
ledgment of our just, our unalterable demands,
which are stated in his proclamation, and to
which Ke-ying is referred ; at the same time assuring him, that the day that would again see the
two nations united in peace would be the happiest
of his life. He concluded by saying, that he
would be delighted to meet so illustrious a person
as accredited plenipotentiary, but must decline

the honour of an interview with any private individual, however high his station.

27th. — Went on shore with Captain Grey to examine a hollow bastion, placed to flank a straight wall on either side: it is pierced with numerous loop-holes, which are made accessible by a spiral staircase: it commands, within a short distance, the spot where our ladders were planted, but, fortunately for our troops, the enemy were dislodged by the Auckland's fire before they were within matchlock range.

Sir Henry has gleaned most important intelligence from papers collected on shore.

Some despatches from the provincial powers to the government do any thing but urge peace, while they own the great distress our ascent and blockade of the river has produced. Others express a fear that we have detached a squadron to blockade the gulf of Petchelee, which the letters say would cause, in addition to the stoppage of this river, utter ruin. While the former continues open, hope remains; for with the S. W. monsoon all supplies, both from the tributaries and the main, can, with a little activity, be landed before winter.

In the evening two white opaque buttoned mandarins came on board the Queen: they were bearers of letters from Elipoo, and were handsome intelligent men, under five and twenty, upwards of six feet high, and stout in proportion.

I was surprised and gratified to see a degree of modesty, blended with proper independence of demeanour, both in their carriage and conversation, the more remarkable in these individuals, as they must be among the exceptions to the sway of example.

2d of August. — I went with a companion to see our horses on board the junk: they are some that the artillery (our never-failing friends) caught running about the town and compounds. They are hardy animals, about the size of a Galloway, and would be, I doubt not, under proper management, very acceptable ponies in any country. Indeed, our short care improved them vastly.

In the afternoon I landed on the north shore with Captain Watson to see some ruined walls. One leaves the shore at right angles, and extends inland for some distance, until lost amid rubbish and underwood, the other runs nearly parallel with the river, diverging from its shores at an acute angle. In some places it is entirely hid by accumulated earth. What caught my attention was its structure of stone — a durable. material not usually employed in this part of China. It may be a portion of the old terrace of the Royal Gardens of Woo-yeun, or, perhaps, the facing to

an old canal now no more.   We might have
arrived at more certain conclusions, if our research
had not been suddenly disturbed by a drove of
ponies galloping past.   We could not resist the
Yorkshireman's propensity, so, converting the
galley's main sheet into a *lazo*, we gave chase.
Watson volunteered to be the *gaucho*, while I offi-
ciated as *haciendou* to guide the direction of the
drove.   After several throws, which displayed
Watson's skill in the *pampa* accomplishment, he
succeeded in catching one round the neck; but
the little brute proved so restive, that the gallant
Captain had to decide between certain damage to
his boat, had he taken it on board, and non-pos-
session of the horse: the first consideration
gained the day, and the pony his—liberty.

3*d*.—Cornwallis.   Recommenced the ascent
of the river, for the purpose of proceeding to
Nanking.   The Vixen took us in tow early in
the forenoon; but the chow-chow water retarded
our progress considerably until we entered the
south arm of the river, which wound near the
base of the chain of mountains to the southward.
A powerful sun shone without the intervention of
a single cloud to protect our craniums.   The
masts of the Dido, the upper guard-ship, soon
hove in sight, and when within four miles of her,
Harry Keppel came on board.   He had the

command of an extensive portion of the river, with two or three small craft under his orders to assist. He has been acting as a commissary as well as magistrate in his proper person, and has supplied more stock than all the fleet together, besides conciliating the good will of the people around him. He told me of the market he had established at the entrance of a large town we saw from the ship; of the fat elder who sought protection from him, and of a most laborious dinner that he sat down to with the officers of his squadron: it consisted of bird's nest soup, shark's fins, and all the other luxuries of the season and country. After the gastronomy was over, the fat gentleman reclined upon a couch properly placed to show the strangers how to smoke opium: his pipe was primed by a lean attendant seated near him.

We anchored shortly after sunset abreast of a hilly ridge, descending abruptly into the river.

4th. — Weighed at daylight; headed a tide of four knots an hour; saw a wretched little cata-maran with a mat sail, and English jack flying, shove off from a junk lying in shore, with the intention of intercepting us; she failed, and the two disconsolate wights, yclept Major M—— and Lieut. E——, fruitlessly held up a large fish as a bribe to heave to — certainly a strong temptation to resist before breakfast.

About five miles from where we weighed, our course varied by degrees from W. N. W. to N. W. by N.; the river then took a bend W. and W. S. W., the waters thrown off the northern shore by the first high land we have met with on that side. Its appearance was cheering; a well regulated variety of hill and dale, diversified by plantations and pasture land, reminded us of our own country and prospects familiar to us all. Without such an occasional reminiscence, it is imposing a tax upon one's memory to compare old scenes with the changing new.

> " 'Tis folly to dream of a bower of green,
>   When there is not a leaf on the tree."

Far to the S. W., about eight miles, we could see for a moment, as we opened a valley between two intervening hills, the famed porcelain pagoda of Nanking, and shortly after the wall, extending, like a huge snake, over hill and over valley, topping the young trees on either side. Three hills, the highest of which I fancy must be 800 feet, flank the eastern wall, outside its circuit, and hide a portion of the S. E. angle from our view, whilst small and steep eminences, clothed with bamboo and underwood, rise directly on the inside of the inner front, forming positions admirably adapted for military defence. The prospect, although not what a Westmoreland or Swiss tourist would think deserving his romantic regard, is, nevertheless, pleasing and fine, and worthy the site of a great capital.

The immense river laves its very walls; the considerable and graceful mountains and extensive plain at their base, upon which the city stands, have all the dignity of size and position to command the respect of the beholder, and to prepare him for the grand dimensions of a great city. On the northern shore is seen a high embattled wall, vying in solidity and extent with that of Nanking; this is said to be the wall of Pou-keou, but I rather think it must be the famous breastwork behind which the victorious Tartar army lay a year encamped, before they crossed the river to attack Nanking. The old camp was afterwards converted into hunting grounds for the conqueror, and still exists, a royal preserve.

CHAP. IX.

At a quarter past 11 A. M., on the 4th of August, 1842, the first European vessel, and that an English 74, anchored off the manned walls of the ancient capital of China.

Triangular flags with waving pennants of the yack ox hair, fluttering above the ramparts, identified the soldiers as Tartars, while their uniforms of bright orange and red denoted them guards from the northern frontiers : fine men they were, and we could see, without the aid of our glasses, three to every embrasure, and all armed with matchlocks. The breastworks had been newly repaired, gingals mounted upon them, besides boxes of lime piled up to throw upon the escalading party.

The portion of the wall we see is upwards of

thirty-five feet in height, built of brick against the escarped sides of the low chain of hills, and protected to the north, west, and south by a deep canal, serving as a wet ditch.

I embarked in the forenoon with the Admiral's party on board one of the small steamers, to make a reconnoissance past the walls of Nanking. The river is divided by a large alluvial island, doubtless formed by an accumulated deposit stopped by the projection upon which the north-western wall stands. We followed the inner branch for about six miles, until we were opposite the south-eastern angle. Upon the high and broad ramparts, and slightly screened by breast-works recently run up, were rows of tents along the greater portion of the line.

From our position we saw but little of the town; but an impulse was given to our curiosity to explore the tempting groves surrounding it by the occasional glimmer through the trees of a gilded pinnacle, or glimpse of a temple, only partially seen.

On our ascent we entrapped a sanpan containing four men; the elder of whom we brought on board to interrogate, and to prevent stoppage, the boat was towed astern. He voluntarily told us that the broken garrison of Chin-kiang-foo had joined this in a most pitiable state; that nearly all were wounded; that the Chinese inhabitants were precluded from passing either in or out of Nanking, and that the canal skirting the southern face was blocked up by sunken junks full of stones. The truth of this information was confirmed by our own observation from the mast-head.

While he was undergoing his examination his companions managed to swamp the boat, by bad steering; the steamer was instantly stopped; the admiral's barge shoved off, saved the crew, righted the sanpan, and within five minutes the dripping Chinese were on board safe and sound; but the old man's wailing was so loud and inconsolable that the Admiral was but too glad to send him away without further questioning.

Upon our arrival at the ship we found the two white-buttoned mandarins our acquaintances of Chin-kiang waiting the Admiral's return: they were the bearers of a despatch from Elipoo, stating that a high dignitary, a relation of the Emperor, in conjunction with himself, was empowered to treat for peace. He regretted our rapid ascent of the river, as he had proceeded some portion of the way to our late anchorage, where he anticipated the pleasure of meeting the high authorities of the honourable nation, and he was now retracing his steps, which, from his indifferent health, he grieved to say, would occupy more time than he could wish.   He again, with great plausibility, enlarged upon the prospects of a long war, depicted the blessings of peace to both nations, and the certain misery that would inevitably befall both conquerors and conquered if hostilities were continued.   He ended by entreating we would wait his arrival.

The messengers had brought presents of fresh tea (very neatly packed in small baskets), sweetmeats, and some pieces of silk.   The latter articles were returned with a " cumshaw" equivalent in value to the things retained.

On the 5th two brass-buttoned mandarins came with a chop from the Governor-general, offering us 300,000 dollars if we would move down the river.   I believe no answer was returned to this.   Shortly after they came back with an offer to double the sum, upon agreement to the same conditions.   Again the same officers came on board with a letter from the Tartar General, proposing an interview with the Commander-in-Chief exclusive of the Plenipotentiary, knowing it was useless to ask him.   It was refused.

A letter delivered at the same time informed Sir Henry that Elipoo had arrived, and had made anxious inquiries after his Excellency's health.

This forenoon I accompanied the Admiral and party in a steamer, to explore a creek which we ascertained cut off the corner round which the great river bends. It skirts within a few hundred yards the site of the old eastern wall (portions of which we could occasionally trace), and forms a semicircular bend from the base of the steep mountain of Chung-shan (the highest of the three already mentioned) until it again joins the main river. We discovered two good landing-places; the one about half way, the other two thirds down. From the former a pathway leads from low swampy ground to a wooded valley between the hills, and the latter is a causeway of importance; a place of traffic directly at the foot of an abrupt and singuarly shaped promontory called Yen-tse-shan, or the Swallow's Nest. A little temple crowns the summit, almost overhanging the perpendicular cliff jutting into the river. When we passed it, it was crowded inside and out with wondering people gaping at the " Demon Ship." A neat village spreads round its base, and rises up the inland slope towards several jos-houses, which are the highest buildings.

A broad paved road leads from the shore, and

passes under an arched gateway that connects two
hills naturally divided by a steep ravine, with a
continuous breadth, and in good repair : this road
traverses a bosky country to within 500 yards of
the walls, and then over paddy and corn land to
the Taiping Gate ; from thence the wall extends
to the southward over a spur of Chung-shan, and
there turns off to the west.   We found the water
in the creeks sufficiently deep for any ship of the
fleet, free from obstructions, and the current inconsiderable.

6*th*. — We are anxiously waiting for the
portion of the transports detained by contrary
winds.

The sickness which began to make sad havoc
with both arms of the force, before we left Ching-
kiang-foo, has not diminished as we thought it
would by change of position.   The flag-ship,
hitherto free, is now under the ban: every pre-
caution that science and cleanliness can effect, in
addition to discipline and occupation, has been
tried, but without avail.   It is hard to reconcile
the fatal progress of pestilence, with the smiling
beauty of so luxuriant a country, and of so clear
and bright a climate.

7*th*. — A day or two ago a despatch from the
Governor-General to the Emperor was intercepted
by one of our vessels stationed a few miles above

the main anchorage. It complained to his majesty that the Supreme General had withdrawn the best troops 500 ly from the city; also that two parties from the captured town of Ching-kiang had entered Nanking, accompanied by numbers of the houseless inhabitants: they reported having fought their way out of the town; that the barbarians had lost many killed, and that if they had been joined by the expected reinforcements, they would, without doubt, have inflicted a severe chastisement upon the rapacious invaders.

8th. — Five mandarins went on board the envoy's steamer with an answer to the letter, in which Sir Henry had agreed to an interview, provided the Chinese commissioners could show the Emperor's authority to enter upon negotiations. It was unsatisfactory; signed by Keying and Elipoo, not as accredited ministers, but simple commissioners limited to treat upon certain subjects, such as future commercial arrangement, and the payment of sums to conclude the war. In making mention of the Queen they placed her rank two grades below the Emperor's.

Sir Henry instantly sent the letter back, pointing out the insult, which he concluded must be a mistake of the secretary who wrote it: he demanded an instant explanation and apology. They must be aware, he wrote, that her Majesty was second to no sovereign on the face of the globe.

An answer full of apologies, and (catching at Sir Henry's hint) accusing the secretary who wrote the letter of ignorance and neglect, and protesting no such error should occur in future, was sent back.

The plenipotentiary declined an interview, and warned the faithless old men that he would not stay hostilities, nor interfere for a single second with the active operations of the Commanders-in-chief.

9th. — Intelligence that the " all spreading General " has entered the city with reinforcements has been communicated through the medium of one of the brass buttons.   Shortly after this they sent to say that Nanking was a poor town, and could not afford to pay more than 300,000 dollars ransom.

10th. — War upon the ascendant.   The last ships of the fleet have arrived.

11th. — Disembarked two large bodies of troops. Lord Saltoun marched from the " Swallow's Nest " — Sir Hugh landed at the centre pathway.   About two hours after their landing a chop was translated, stating that Elipoo and his colleague had received full powers to treat upon every subject, and beseeching a suspension of operations.   Not to be thought of; so on we marched up the valley and over the low ground, extending between the river and the S.E. wall. The country most lovely. For two miles and a half we traversed thickets of pomegranates, Spanish chestnuts, plantations of trembling beech, and a long fibred fir — a much prized wood used for building junks. An occasional open space displayed fields in a high state of cultivation, producing the capsicum, the pumpkin, the melon, and the bringall, also the large leafed tobacco plant; the various compounds and divisions bordered by the stately tassel grass, waving its silky plume to every passing breeze. At intervals we could see the walls, and sometimes stopped to reconnoitre; but until we ascended a conical hill, higher than the rest, and close to the edge of the level lying between us and the city, we were able to take no good survey.

The prospect from this summit was very fine, no feature grand, but altogether very picturesque and striking. To the right of where we stood, round wooded eminences extended in detached hillocks, rather than ridges, to the river, while to the left in the same way, but with more developement of size and feature, they rose towards the last and highest of the range, Chung-shan. In front the plain sloped, rich in produce, to the vast

Babylonian wall; the summit of which preserved its horizontal level, notwithstanding the great irregularity of ground, which is so considerable, that in some places the rampart must be ninety feet in height.

We could discern the paved causeway leading from the pass of the " Swallow's Nest," extending over the plain to the Taiping Gate, which is at the corner of an angle of the wall nearly opposite to where we stood, and close to the inner wall surrounding the Tartar portion of the city. Directly in front of us a projecting bastion flanked by inner works seemed, from the firmness of the ground and comparative lowness of the ramparts, a likely spot to escalade ; accordingly, twenty men and an officer under the command of Captain Pears of the Madras Engineers, were sent to reconnoitre, and Lieut. Heatly, Deputy-Assistant-Adjutant-General, and I, went with them. Brushwood covered our progress up to a small village which extended in a single street from the wall, and lay exposed to the fire of the garrison. Pears left the men under cover of the houses, and proceeded in company with Heatly and myself down the street in full view of the troops upon the wall, who no sooner observed us than they assembled in great numbers from the extended posts ; but seeing that we were unattended, they allowed us to walk all round the bastion, and make every observation without hinderance or molestation. We addressed them in the few words of Chinese we knew, but could not elicit, nor in fact did we wait long for a reply, and after we had seen all that was necessary, we left them standing with their matchlocks and bows in their hands.

In the mean time the General had observed the rush made upon our first appearance, and had ordered the Grenadiers under arms to our rescue; fortunately, however, their assistance was not required. On our return the General prepared to visit Lord Saltoun's position: he was posted with two regiments and artillery upon the plain to the south of our hill, which Sir Hugh left in possession of H. M.'s 26th, with orders to garrison the jos house, hitherto the salubrious abode of some fifteen lazy priests of Fo.

After a hot march of two miles, we arrived amongst straggling houses completely deserted; the doors shut and fastened; and over their portals we observed large red paper placards inscribed with black characters, signifying " submissive people."

We found Lord Saltoun in an extensive building off the main street, surrounded by his troops. We then retraced our steps to the steamer, and were

on board in time for the all-important daily occupation — dinner.

12th. — Last night I slept on board the junk
in which Major Malcolm came up the river.   A
great transformation had been effected since I,
with him, first boarded her, lying among the
crowd of other junks up the Blonde's creek; then
several cribs, like those in Highland cabins, with
sliding panels, expressly constructed to destroy
health by excluding the fresh air of heaven, were
built between the two main cabins, and every
little recess converted, with elaborate ingenuity,
into stow-holes — a description of repository the
Chinese are very partial to.   These were now all
cleared away, and in their room stood a mag-
nificently carved cabinet, nearly the height of the
cabin: it was placed against the bulk-head, and
stocked for our daily use with china that a connois-
seur would have envied; silk curtains, graced with
trellised shutters; tables and chairs, books and papers, were in due proportion, and two camp beds,
which in the daytime supplied the place of sofas.
The kitchen was abaft, and most satisfactory meals
our Chinese cooks concocted in it.   Here was a
complete floating establishment, which we could
convey with us to any spot we pleased. Our crew
consisted of five Chinese, including the original
captain: we had besides two English seamen to

keep watch, and act, in case of necessity, as a
body guard: two Chinese servants and ourselves
completed the establishment.

Now for her equipment: —she had two masts,
both before the central section, and both inclining
forward; no rigging on either; nothing to support them but the pair of single halyards to hoist
the sails; and their purchase could be doubled
and trebled with great ease by a most ingenious
toggle purchase. The sails were of cotton, stretched
upon bamboos. From the after-end of each a sheet
rove through a dead block, forming an extensive
crow-foot. Each space between the bamboos comprised a reef, which could be taken in on the
instant by lowering the halyards to the proper
distance: the anchors were iron grappling. The
cables made of bamboo strips, beautifully plaited
and perfectly round, were very buoyant and
elastic: the smoothness of their surface prevents
the liability of chafing, and their great buoyancy
would render them eminently useful for warping,
even in our own service. The rudder was passed
up through a hole in the overhanging transom,
and the keel, confined by two keel ropes, passed
under the bottom, and fastened to bollards abreast
the main-mast. Such are the fittings of our craft
and the generality of Chinese junks. We found
it in the hands of its habitual proprietors manage-

able enough ; less so than a floating haystack in our own.

We landed our ponies, and shortly after dawn joined our three high authorities at the centre landing-place. We mustered a large party, and proceeded to the hill, where the 26th Regt. were quartered, as the General was desirous to point out the spot where he intended to commence his attack. On our way we met a litter conveying a wounded soldier of the 26th to the beach. He, poor fellow, was startled in the night by loud cries from among his comrades that the Chinese were upon them : he rushed out in his shirt, and was received upon the bayonet of the sentry at the entrance, who unfortunately heard the disturbance, and mistook the white figure running towards him in a loose robe for a Chinese. A young recruit, in the activity of his dreams, had caused the alarm.

We reached our military post with excellent appetites, which we satisfied with beef steaks from a cow we found the day before stowed away among some high reeds.

CHAP. X.

CHINESE OFFICIAL CORRESPONDENCE. — THE PAWNBROKER OF YANG-CHOW. — CONFERENCES WITH THE DEPUTIES. — RESPECT PAID TO THE IMPERIAL EDICTS. — EXCURSION ALONG THE BANKS OF THE CANAL. — FLOODS. — CLIMATE. — THUNDER-STORM. — THE BAMBOO. — FIRST INTERVIEW WITH IMPERIAL COMMISSIONERS.

3d of August. — BREAKFASTED with Sir Henry, who showed me some papers which had fallen into his hands, detailing an admirable official system, which the Chinese practise, of having at the supreme boards of the various departments particular envelopes appropriate to each office, and marked in accordance with the subject of the papers they contain. They are filed and numbered, and kept in presses under the immediate charge of the minister, who imposes the same responsibility on the local governors, to whom they are sent, as he is under to his Imperial master for their safety.

While I was on board the Queen, the old pawnbroker of Yang-chow arrived with a letter. This is the man who, to save his city (which is situated upon the banks of the canal, on the north side of the river) from assault, collected among his fellow-townsmen a ransom of 500,000 dollars. Such a compromise would, a few months ago, have cost him either his life or liberty; but in this instance he has been rewarded with a blue button, and an order has lately been sent him from Pekin to endeavour to negotiate a like arrangement for Nanking, — a strong evidence that the Imperial government has, at last, been forced into the conviction that its greatest and strongest towns are at our mercy.

Both yesterday and to-day Major Malcolm, the Secretary of Legation, has, with Mr. Morrison, had preliminary interviews with the provincial treasurer and Tartar General to examine the alleged Imperial authority, and also to discuss and gain the consent of the Commissioners to the outline of the treaty drawn up by Sir Henry for their inspection; so that when the high functionaries of both nations meet, no difference may arise to mar or interrupt what they themselves term "the smooth stream of good understanding."

Malcolm's interview of this morning was most unsatisfactory: they would not produce the Imperial commission, but only a partial copy, nor would they come to any definite arrangement upon any single point; so he left them with the clear understanding that the guns now in po-

sition would open fire at day-dawn if the Plenipotentiary had not the authority to show the
Commanders-in-chief before that time.   This produced the desired result.   Mandarins came off,
after midnight, with a letter from Ke-ying, beseeching that another interview might be arranged for the following day, when the Imperial
commission would be produced.

14*th.* — After breakfast I accompanied Major
Malcolm and Messrs. Morrison and Thom on
shore to the interview, which was to decide
whether the Chinese would yield to our demands.

It took place in a large temple situated in the
suburbs under the south wall, and a short distance from the canal up which we proceeded
in the Queen's cutter, by an opening cut
through heavy rafts of timber drawn across its
entrance to block up the passage.   Several large
junks full of stones had also been sunk athwart
ships, but these were burst and broken up into
various portions by the strength of the current,
leaving ample room for an unobstructed onward
progress to the largest boat.

We landed on a rickety bamboo pier constructed for our accommodation, and were instantly surrounded by a crowd composed of the
lowest order, who appeared eager to see specimens of the formidable "barbarians;" and the

sight to men, who judge by size and muscle, must have been humiliating to their self-love, as we were all of slight build, and, moreover, had come quite unprepared for the show.   Linen clean, I hope, but for weeks unacquainted with either iron or mangle ; shoes that would have done good service on the moors, and coats of modest cut and old acquaintance, with the exception of the gallant Secretary's gaily braided affair (which, by the by, was most unhappily contrasted with his nether garments).   Two of the party, if not all four, were under thirty, — an age in a Chinaman's eyes undeserving of respect.

We were received at the entrance of the spacious court of the temple by a bevy of mandarins, from the blue to the brass button.   Different from us, they rustled in embroidered silks and flowered muslin of a design and beauty of texture worthy even to deck the forms of our own fair dames.   They marshalled us with many obsequious bows, and really much graceful courtesy, into the great hall of audience, where Mr. Secretary "Whang" and the Tartar General "Chin" were standing to receive us.   After Mr. Morrison had severally introduced us, we sat down in chairs that would have held two Daniel Lamberts, round a square table, Whang opposite Malcolm, I next to Chin, and Mr. Thom opposite me.

Mr. Morrison retired to another table to translate some papers.

Whang, a man of seven or eight and thirty, is considered one of the most rising statesmen in China, and his manners and conversation marked him a perfect gentleman. I do not remember ever having met, even in my own country, a person of more gentle and polished manner or courteous breeding than this Chinese, so different from the majority of his countrymen in their intercourse with foreigners. The General was a portly old veteran of about sixty, wearing a little grey tufted beard, a plain dress, crystal ball, and peacock's feather. His red ball had been taken away for some offence shortly before our arrival.

The other mandarins stood round among the servants, and listened, as is the universal custom, to all that was discussed.

At the door were a few peace-keepers or police, wearing red felt conical caps, each topped with a cock's feather, which traversed round upon a swivel. They were armed with cow-hide whips, which they kept in pretty frequent use upon the shoulders of the pressing and chattering rabble outside.

While Mr. Morrison was transcribing copies of his papers, tea was handed round by the attendants, and whether drank or not, a hot cup every two or three minutes superseded the colder beverage.

When the writing was finished, Malcolm produced the patent from her Majesty appointing him Secretary of Legation: this was to show that he was the accredited and proper person to negotiate on the part of the Envoy. After this was looked at, he displayed Sir Henry Pottinger's, which was translated *verbatim* by Mr. Thom, and the Queen's seal and signature pointed out to the deputies.

Major Malcolm then demanded to see the Emperor's commission, which, after some little delay and great ceremony, was brought forth from a chest by a mandarin, under whose special charge it appeared to be. He carried the roll of yellow silk in both his hands, and proceeded — his eyes reverentially fixed upon it — with slow and solemn steps towards the table, and placed it in the hands of Whang with tenderness and forced resignation. The produce of the silk wrapper was a little shabby yellow box badly made and worse painted, containing the power, which Morrison on examination pronounced, as far as he was able to judge, authentic.

I was greatly amused watching the anxious and horrified faces of the various Chinese when Mr. Morrison touched the commission, and I thought the old keeper would have fainted on the spot when he, for an instant, held it in one hand.

In China the same respect is paid to an Imperial edict, or the mark of the vermilion pencil, that, with us, the sovereign only receives in person. There are many powers delegated by sign manual throughout the empire, and in these cases the same homage is bestowed upon the written name of the Emperor, that is, in other countries, only yielded to the prince himself. *

After our skeleton treaty was satisfactorily arranged, and written both in Chinese and English, one copy being kept by the mandarins, the other by Malcolm, for Sir Henry's inspection, we rose to depart, and the old General laughingly remarked that the conditions were hard, but, after all, were only what they would have demanded under similar circumstances; that a war between nations might be likened to a game of chance, in which the loser must pay the winner ; that this time they were the unfortunates, from having neglected the art of war during centuries of peace and prosperity; that our ships were our stronghold and glory, and had proved their curse.

In the evening I landed my pony, and rode along the north bank of the canal for two miles,

* See Appendix.

in company with Dr. Woosnam. Owing to the
lowness of their situation, the cottages which
we saw were half flooded, and we surprised the
few remaining wretched inhabitants sitting before
their doors, after their day's labour in the paddy
fields, eating their evening meal. They sat stu-
pified and still as we passed, perhaps thinking
(and with justice) that no one, however reckless,
would take the trouble to molest either themselves
or dwellings which could produce so little.

We turned an angle, and could see for a considerable distance along the extensive canal skirting the south-western wall. Several small punts
and fishing canoes were gliding about close to the
tall rushes, and a few old salt junks lay moored
along the shores, mastless and decayed.

We went to an isolated farm-house, built on a
knoll of ground somewhat higher than the surrounding land, to light

> " Sublime tobacco, which from east to west
>   Cheers the tar's labours, and the Turkman's rest,"

and saw evident marks of a flood having covered
at least four feet of its walls, in which case the
whole surrounding flat, from the walls of Nanking to the river, must have been entirely under
water, and this we afterwards ascertained to have
been the fact. They say that for the last ten
years the farmers of the low lands have had to

live in boats during several months of each season
after the rains.

No people can be healthy who reside, as these
do, in the midst of the extensive decay of vegetable
matter which perpetually succeeds the rapid eva-
poration of stagnant water; nor are they : putrid
fevers, cholera, and ague have, within the last few
years, carried off multitudes.

15th. — As the day broke, the stillness of
the heavy atmosphere became disturbed by fitful gusts from the northern hills, and the sky,
for the first time since we anchored here, was
overcast with heavy masses of leaden-coloured
clouds, indicating, by their rapidly increasing den-
sity, a speedy thunder-storm, — an event long
wished for, as the only hope to stay the still
increasing cholera, by freeing the air from the
load of electric fluid.

It has long been a disputed point whether this
fatal illness is produced and spread by such a
state of the atmosphere, or by other causes
common to infection, nor do I, who am no judge,
venture to assert an opinion; but it is a fact well
worthy of attention, that the surgeon of the flag-
ship, Dr. King, distinctly felt, in two instances,
a shock resembling that from a galvanic battery
on touching the pulses of the patients.

Our predictions were realised: thunder and

lightning, with heavy rain, lasted for about three hours, leaving the atmosphere light and the air cool and refreshing. The clouds rolled back to the verge of the distant horizon, and the evening sun shone with a tempered heat, more congenial than it had hitherto been.

In no other portion of the globe have I ever felt the temperature so oppressive as in this, or so enervating in its effects on the energies both of mind and body; and not even in more tropical regions are the alternations so rapid and capricious. Upon any change of wind from the regular monsoon (affected by such causes as the above storm), the thermometer will fall 12° in an hour; and a southerly breeze, on the other hand, at this season, will raise it from its fall to 130° on the hill-side or open plain, filling the air at the same time with a weight of vapour from the moistened flats, which, during the nights, again descends in heavy dews upon the thick grass and abundant foliage, thus keeping it in perpetual verdure.

All the central provinces are comparatively champaign country, consisting of damp alluvial loam, from which a constant vapour exhales in sufficient quantity to destroy the freshness of the southern monsoon.

The land and sea breezes that render the temperature of islands close to, and upon the equator, delightful even to Europeans, are of course unknown in the interior of China, where the air becomes sluggish by passing for hundreds of miles over plains teeming with vegetation, unbroken by any mountainous ridge, whose snowy summits might distribute healthy and refreshing gales.

16*th*. — To-day was the day appointed for the first grand interview; but owing to the time required to write out our demands in Chinese, review expressions, and so forth, it has unavoidably been postponed.

In the forenoon I landed with Captain Trowbridge and Mr. Lay at the centre landing-place; the latter to collect insects and butterflies, while we shot snipes.

We ranged among deserted cottages and secluded glens, hitherto unvisited by any European. There is something in this reflection which always excites an alertness of observation, even when there may be but little to satisfy the curiosity; and in this case the withdrawal of one's thoughts from the busy scenes we left behind, to the close examination of quiet, tranquil, and beautiful nature, was beyond belief pleasurable.

The clean weeding of the fields, where we met with them in the level bottoms of some of the broader valleys, led to the conclusion that the labourers lay concealed in the vicinity. We strolled to one very lovely spot — a little basin. On its south side rose a round, happy-looking hill, clothed with trees and shrubs — birch, fir, ash, and the arbutus — from among which grey rocks of granite protruded, half covered by flowering creepers. We stood in the centre of a field of melons. A little further on, on the same level, a grove of chestnut and palm trees concealed the opening into our retreat, while to the north, opposite the hill, a large grove of bamboos — the queen of all graceful plants — shot up straight stems, their head shoots drooping like plumes of feathers.

The Chinese have written as many rhapsodies to the bamboo as to ladies' eye-brows — a favourite theme of celebration—and by so doing they merely evince a proper sense of gratitude; for without this most useful vegetable a Chinaman would be as helpless as he would be without his chopsticks.

The bamboo furnishes both food and raiment, the uprights of their houses, the beams, chairs, tables, screens, mats, flower-stands, water-wheels, drinking-cups, powder-horns, bottles, hats, baskets, pumps, bellows, spears, sails, ropes, and many other things, which, to enumerate, would fill a page.

Soup can be made from the shoots; for, as
the story goes *, " Măng Tsung, who lived in
the Tsin dynasty, when young, lost his father,
his mother was very sick ; and one winter's day
she longed to taste a soup of bamboo sprouts,
but Măng could not procure any. At last, he
went into the grove of bamboos, clasped the trees
with his hands, and wept bitterly. His filial
affection moved Nature, and the ground slowly
opened, sending forth several shoots, which he
gathered and carried home. He made soup of
them, of which his mother ate, and immediately
recovered from her malady."

There are numbers of these stories written
for the benefit of the rising generation.

We returned on board without adventure.

17*th*. — Another change of wind, and some
more heavy rain; diplomacy at a stand still, and,
for a wonder, on our side. The Chinese are
anxious and pressing to patch up differences, and
have the river open ; but it is necessary that great
care should be taken in the wording of our full
demands — Mr. Morrison's present difficult task
— as, he says, the omission of a single syllable
might change the entire sense of the sentence.

They do not conceal from us now their great

* Chinese Repos. Example of Filial Duty.

anxiety for the speedy termination of the war.
Anarchy, discontent, and open revolt are daily
increasing; nor can the lawless outrages committed in the interior, by the gathering hordes
of plunderers, be suppressed until the garrisons
are left free to act, by a settlement with us.

18*th*. — The breezes are moderate, and the
weather cloudy. Our demands were sent late
last night : — to-day they offered to embark one
million and a half of dollars, which Sir Henry
refused to receive until the treaty was signed.

They seem to think that money is our only
consideration — as the great "rebel-quelling General Yih-shan" wrote in his memorial to the
Emperor that "commerce is to these foreigners
the very artery of life:"— perhaps it is a disagreeable fact.

Malcolm met the delegates on board the Blonde
this afternoon for the last time. He told them
to inform the Imperial Commissioners that Sir
Henry would be ready for a conference to-
morrow, on board the Cornwallis, and that the
day after he would return their visit within the
walls of Nanking. To this latter arrangement
they, in evident trepidation, instantly objected,
alleging, as an excuse, that they could not depend on the forbearance of the Tartar troops,
all of whom were exasperated against us for

former defeats, and might do us harm; that if, on the other hand, we were accompanied by a strong guard, say 1000 men, an ebullition of feeling might excite a collision, and thereby effectually destroy the present promising appearances of a peaceful and lasting arrangement of all our difficulties; so this question is left for the present *in statu quo.*

19*th.* — The auspicious day has at last arrived, when, as the Chinese say, " the powerful of nations are to meet and exchange the fiery eye of vindictiveness for the smile of kindness, and the red hand of hostility for the white wand of amity."

Between 11 and 12 A. M. the quarter-deck of the flag ship presented an unusual glitter: gay uniforms of blue and scarlet in their first freshness after months of veiled brightness had superseded the honest habiliments of service dye. A captain's guard was under arms, life lines on the yards, and the little Medusa steamer off the canal — all to do honour to our expected visiters. Three guns, the Chinese royal salute, were to be fired upon the embarkation of the Commissioners from the wharf, and at the mouth of the canal Commander Richards of the Cornwallis was stationed to take them from their unwieldy conveyance to the Medusa.

The guns at last announced the long-expected moment; and we could sometimes see, between the trees and houses, banners, streamers, and silk umbrellas waving about as the boat floated down the stream.

Getting into the steamer, shod in their thick Tartar boots, was to them a service of danger, and which caused considerable delay. At last they paddled up and came alongside from the steamer in the Admiral's barge. The yards were manned, guard presented arms, drums beat, band played, and the Plenipotentiary, between the two Commanders-in-chief, received Ke-ying, Elipoo, and New-king the viceroy of the two Yieng provinces, and Commander-in-chief of all their armies.

A number of subordinate officers and attendants, besides three or four mandarins whom we knew from having been brought in contact with them at Chusan and Ning-po, followed in their wake. They presented in their flowing robes a lively contrast to our close fitting and (I think) ungraceful dress.

After a few of us had been presented the authorities entered the Admiral's cabin, and were ushered to a large sofa, placed to face forwards, so that they might see every body and every thing. Sir Henry sat on the left — the Chinese seat of honour — the General on the right, and the Admiral as the host, I think, next to him. Tea, coffee, wine, sweetmeats, and cherry brandy were handed round, the last of which they greatly appreciated.

As this was merely intended to be a visit of ceremony, no questions relative to future arrangements were mooted.

Ke-ying evinced considerable interest in all he saw, although he never trespassed on good breeding, or forgot what was due to his dignity, by asking questions. Elipoo, who was upwards of eighty, appeared fatigued, and his countenance bore a sad expression of mental suffering, which is not to be wondered at, poor old man, considering the many misfortunes and heavy displeasure of his Imperial master, that had arisen to him out of his former intercourse with us.

New-king sat without showing any outward or visible sign, beyond an occasional smack of satisfaction after each glass of cherry brandy.

The General was as loquacious as on the first occasion that I saw him, and pretended a great interest in, and examined with a critical inquisitiveness, every thing appertaining to the art of war. The band elicited very great attention. The attendants outside were not so well mannered as their masters : they became trouble-

some and familiar, after their short-lived bashful-
ness had worn off.

The Commissioners, at the Admiral's invitation,
walked round the various decks; and I was
somewhat amused to see that the men, to make
their messes look the smarter, had decorated the
shelves with small jos-images and a few other
articles of choice taste that they had picked up
in their perambulations. Well might the Chinese
have exclaimed with Samson,

> " O indignity ! O blot
> To honour and religion ! "

But they acted the wiser part of " laissez faire,
laissez passer ; " and even their noisy train were by
humbled vanity recalled to a temporary sense of
decorum.

No very marked interest was shown for any
thing but the music, which surprised me the
more, as both Sir John Barrow and Lord
Jocelyn particularly mention their apathy and
want of taste for harmony.

They left the ship as they came, and highly
pleased at their reception.

CHAP. XI.

TRIP TO THE DIDO. — SECOND INTERVIEW WITH COMMIS-
SIONERS.

20th of August.—I EMBARKED at daylight in a boat
to proceed to the Dido, at anchor about twenty-
five miles down the river — a little more than half
way between Chin-kiang-foo and Nanking.

The weather which had been foul all night
cleared towards morning, and in a boat the clouds
were preferable to a hot sun.   A pleasant sail of
three hours carried me alongside.

I found my old shipmates suffering from fever
and ague, the prevailing disease.   They told me
that for some days past they had remarked many
headless bodies floating past them ; these probably
were plunderers beheaded by the mandarins.

I shoved off about sunset to return to the
Cornwallis — a most tedious undertaking, with
a strong contrary current, and a foul wind against
us.   About 9 P.M., after crossing the river, I
anchored close to the shore to rest the men.   An
hour before daylight we again weighed — the
same foul wind brought down masses of black
clouds, which soon opened their torrents upon
us ; we had to anchor to hold our own ; and I

sat for two hours under the heaviest thunder-storm it had ever been my lot to encounter, contemplating my saturated books and baggage.

The current was hourly increasing in velocity from the down-rush of the upland rains and the eddies of still water close to the rushes decreasing in proportion to the river's rise ; so we had nothing for it but to make the essay, and for eight miles along the even bank of a straight reach we had inch by inch to strain our way.

> " So the boat's brawny crew the currents stem,
>   And slow advancing struggle with the stream ;
>   But if they slack their hands or cease to strive,
>   Then down the flood with headlong haste they drive."
>   DRYDEN.

This was literally our case, and a most disagreeable one it was — foul winds, and a strong current over twenty miles of ground.

By noon we doubled the point of the straight reach, and stopped to rest at a jos house, where we found some tea and a fire to warm us. I fancy we were the first of our countrymen that had landed at this place, as we perceived the women and children in the adjoining village busy in their ordinary pursuits.

We entered the Swallow's Nest creek by three P.M., and I remained on board H. M.'s brig Algerine all night, instead of toiling the remaining six miles to the Cornwallis.

22*d*. — The day appointed to return the visit of the Commissioners, who were to receive us in the temple where we first met their delegates.

At 10 A. M. about forty boats shoved off from different ships full of officers of both services, all dressed in their full uniforms.

The Admiral's barge containing the Plenipotentiary and the two Commanders-in-chief took the lead — the others followed as they best could. Vast numbers of Chinese lined the banks of the canal, and accompanied us in their punts.

We landed at a wooden jetty thrown out for the purpose, and passed under a bamboo gate, decorated with a few red flags.

When our authorities stepped on shore three guns were fired, to announce their arrival to the Commissioners : they then entered sedan chairs, and were escorted by subordinate mandarins to the temple. About a dozen other chairs were in attendance, and to them a charge was made by officers of all ranks resembling in dignity and activity that which the members of the House of Commons occasionally make into the House of Lords, when they are summoned there to hear an address from the throne — the younger, and consequently the junior officers, gained the day,

The Commissioners received Sir Henry Pottin-

ger and the Commanders-in-chief at the entrance
of the court-yard, and led them between ranks
of unarmed Chinese soldiers, clothed in new uniforms, while the Plenipotentiary's guard of honour,
formed of the grenadier company of the 18th
Royal Irish, and drawn up in front, presented
arms.   The band of the same regiment struck up
" Garryowen," while the penny-trumpets and
hurdy-gurdys of the Chinese were in full force;
but the drummer with the big drum, who had an
ear for music, took care we should not hear a
single note of the tune they played.

Two large apartments were prepared, and tables
spread with piles of sweetmeats.   Chairs placed
in the form of a horse-shoe stood round the tables,
while the centre ones, occupied by our chiefs,
were elevated above the others.

Our vanity prompted us to think that the
Chinese could not feel much humiliation at having
been conquered by the description of men they
this day saw before them : there were upwards of
one hundred and thirty officers, besides the guard,
which was worthy of the distinguished regiment
it belonged to.

This visit passed off in the same manner as the
first; namely, in drinking tea, asking questions,
and making complimentary speeches.

The rooms were hung with festoons of embroidered cloth; round horn lanterns, as large as half-hogsheads, made of one entire piece *, prettily painted and decorated with strings of beads, and hung from the roof. The floors were carpeted with red drugget, and the tables and chairs covered with scarlet cloth richly embroidered with silk.

The numerous mandarins were plainly dressed, which caused an inquiry on the part of the Envoy, and apologies from the Commissioners, who asserted that the rapid dance we had led them prevented them carrying an extensive wardrobe. This could not have been true, as they travelled by water, and brought with them large establishments.

23*d*. — The Chinese are gaining confidence, and abundance of bullocks have been, by request, sent to the fleet: they are fatter, and apparently of a different and a finer breed, than those we ourselves have at different times procured.

26*th*. — This was the day fixed upon for the interview between Sir Henry Pottinger and the Commissioners, to discuss and finally arrange the conditions of the treaty.

The Plenipotentiary and his suite, consisting of Major Malcolm, Doctor Woosnam, Messrs.

---

* The separate pieces of horn are consolidated by the action of heat.

Morrison, Gutzlaff, and Thom (the three interpreters), besides Mr. Eastwick, a friend of Sir
Henry's, and myself, proceeded in the Admiral's
barge up the canal to the appointed landing
place, where we were met by a detachment of
Tartar cavalry and a number of mandarins of
rank. Horses provided by the artillery were in
waiting, as also the Envoy's guard of honour.

Sir Henry landed under a salute of three guns,
and a band struck up which set our teeth on
edge. The horse artillery admirably mounted
upon Arabs preceded the Plenipotentiary, while
the Tartar cavalry brought up the rear, their
silk gowns and shaggy ponies offering a striking
contrast to our fine fellows. We entered the first
gate we came to, opening to the N. W., and
passed for about a mile up a long street leading
to the southward, after which we turned to the
left, and, lastly, to the right into the street where
the large government building, appropriated to
the interview, was plainly observable from the
numerous flags and mandarins in front of it.

Without dismounting, Sir Henry was conducted up the long enclosed entrance of the outer
court, and up the steps of the second (a royal
honour) to the door of the third, where the
Imperial Commissioners were standing, surrounded
by their high officers and functionaries. We

I

were received with much dignified courtesy, and
conducted through several rooms and passages of
this immense house into the chamber of audience
— a square apartment, partitioned by a horse-shoe
railing, round which were placed chairs fronting
tables, loaded with sweetmeats of every description.   The tables and chairs were covered with
red embroidered drapery, and the floor with
crimson drugget. The bottom of this room opened
into a court which was canopied by a chequered
silk awning.

A more tolerable band than we had yet heard
commenced, as we sat down, a tune resembling a
pibroch, and continued to play throughout the
repast.   Young white-buttoned mandarins handed
round tea, hot wine, and sweetmeats, while a
conversation upon general subjects was maintained between the Commissioners and Sir Henry
through the medium of the interpreters.

Numerous patties of minced meat, pork, arrow
root, vermicelli soup, with meat in it, pig's ear
soup, and other strange dishes, were served in
succession, in small china and silver basins, and in
proportion to our various capabilities in making
these messes disappear, we seemed to rise in the
estimation of the beholders.   But human nature
could not support this ordeal long, and, as a *coup
de grace,* Ke-ying insisted upon Sir Henry opening

his mouth while he with great dexterity shot into it several immense sugar-plums.   I shall never forget Sir Henry's face of determined resignation after he found remonstrances were of no avail; nor the figure of Ke-ying, as he stood planted before him, in the attitude of a short-sighted old lady threading a needle, poising the *bonne bouche* between his finger and thumb preparatory to his successful throw.

After this the tables were cleared and business commenced.

The demands, written in both languages, were again read; and, with the exception at first of a slight demur at our detention of Chusan as a guarantee until the full payment of the 21,000,000 of dollars, and a wish to exclude Foo-choo-foo from free trade, were unanimously agreed to.   The commissioners were made perfectly to understand that the final settlement of the tariff, residence of English families in the various towns and their vicinities, the future management of commerce through our own consuls, and the entire abolition of the Hong monopoly, were points only delayed in consequence of the time it would require to discuss their minutiæ in detail, but that they were of such vital importance that if, when they were brought forward, any procrastination or refusal should occur, it would effectually interrupt the amity so auspiciously commenced between the two empires.

None of the critical examination into phrases or expressions, so keenly canvassed and suspiciously viewed by European diplomatists, occupied a moment of their attention. All their anxiety, which was too powerful to be concealed, was centred upon the one main object — our immediate departure; in consequence, almost in the same breath with their assent, they requested the Plenipotentiary to remove the ships away from the canals and to send them down the river. To this the Envoy replied that, upon the treaty being signed, the blockade would be removed, and when the last dollar of the first instalment of six millions was paid, every town and fort within the Yang-tze-kiang would be delivered back into their hands.

Sir Henry then remarked, that as every difference was satisfactorily arranged, he was anxious to say a few words upon a subject — the great cause that produced the disturbances which led to the war — he meant the trade in opium. When this was translated, they unanimously declined entering upon the subject, until Sir Henry assured them he did not wish to speak of it but as a topic of private conversation. They then evinced much interest, and eagerly requested to

know why we would not act fairly towards them,
by prohibiting the growth of the poppy in our
dominions, and thus effectually stop a traffic so
pernicious to the human race. This, he said, in
consistency with our constitutional laws, could
not be done; and he added, that even if England
chose to exercise so arbitrary a power over her
tillers of the soil, it would not check the evil so
far as they (the Chinese) were concerned, while
the cancer remained uneradicated among themselves, but that it would merely throw the market
into other hands.

It, in fact, he said, rests entirely with your-
selves. If your people are virtuous, they will
desist from the evil practice; and if your officers
are incorruptible, and obey their orders, no opium
can enter your country. The discouragement of
the growth of the poppy in our territories rests
principally with you, for nearly the entire produce
cultivated in India travels east to China; if, however, the habit has become a confirmed vice, and
you feel convinced that your power is at present
inadequate to stay its indulgence, you may rest assured your people will procure the drug in spite of
every enactment; would it not, therefore, be better
at once to legalise its importation, and by thus
securing the co-operation of the rich, and of your
authorities, from whom it would thus no longer

be debarred, thereby greatly limit the facilities which now exist for smuggling?

They owned the plausibility of the argument, but expressed themselves persuaded that their Imperial master would never listen to a word upon the subject.

To convince them that what he said was not introduced from any sinister wish to gain an end more advantageous to ourselves, he drew a rapid sketch of England's rise and progress from a barbarous state to a degree of wealth and civilisation unparalleled in the history of the world; which rapid rise was principally attributable to benign and liberal laws, aided by commerce, which conferred power and consequence. He then casually mentioned instances of governments having failed to attain their objects by endeavouring to exclude any particular article of popular desire: tobacco was one of those he alluded to; and now that it was legalised, not only did it produce a large revenue to the crown, but it was more moderately indulged in in Britain than elsewhere.

Mr. Gutzlaff, a perfect master of the Chinese language, was the interpreter, and performed his part well. The Commissioners and surrounding mandarins seemed greatly interested.

The Plenipotentiary also said, that he thought it

probable that, upon the return of the treaty from England, an envoy might be deputed to Pekin, and he wished to know if he would be received with satisfaction and proper respect?

Ke-ying immediately replied with earnestness, that he was sure the Emperor would be very glad to receive an embassy, and took that opportunity to express his sorrow at the treatment Lord Amherst had met with, which he stated was caused by the machinations of a corrupt set of ministers then in office.

Shortly after this we took our leave; and when Sir Henry mounted another salute was fired from two rude pieces about the size of 4-pounders, made from iron bars, hooped together and planted perpendicularly on their breech. The crowd was greater than upon our approach, but silent and orderly.

Elipoo, who appeared very weak and unwell during the conference, requested Dr. Woosnam to prescribe for him. It appeared that, added to old age, he was suffering from violent attacks of fever, ague, and the liver; and from these he desired to be speedily relieved. The doctor said he would prepare medicines if a messenger was sent to the ships with us to take them back. Accordingly a mandarin of the name of Chang, a notorious drunkard, was ordered to accompany us.

CHAP. XII.

28*th of August.* — LAST night Captains Boucher
and Watson of the Blonde and Modeste, with
Lieut. Hall of the Nemesis, Mr. Eastwick and
myself, rode over to the artillery camp, four miles
through a pretty country, with woody knolls and
valleys rich with gardens and fields of grain and
vegetables. For a time we rode by the side of
the moat and fine old wall, and occasionally
through shady lanes, not unlike those in our own
country.

At 4 A. M. we started for the porcelain pagoda,
one of the most celebrated shrines and tallest
towers in China. Our party consisted of twenty-
five, besides a host of servants and coolies ; and,
as one of our number remarked, looked so formidable, that, as we passed beneath the walls, soldiers
were seen hurrying to close the gates and man the
ramparts.

The morning was delightful — a true eastern sun-rise —

> " Clothing the palpable and the familiar
> With golden exhalations of the dawn."

We were mounted upon ponies brought from Amoy and Chin-kiang-foo, strong, sure-footed animals, and vastly improved since they had fallen into our hands.

After riding over a plain of paddy fields, and through a village situated at the entrance to a defile, and partially screened by trees, we ascended the ridge of an eminence (three and a half miles from camp) commanding the N. E. angle of the wall, whence we viewed the Tartar quarter of the city. A second wall surrounds the space where formerly stood the royal palace and gardens, now the Tartar garrison — the houses are almost hid by foliage. Beyond the inner wall we saw but few Chinese houses.

Proceeding onwards we came upon a burial ground situated at the corner of a vast plain, bounded on the one side by the spreading base of the hill from which we had descended, and facing the walls of the capital. Near the foot of the grassy slope, at about the centre of the hill, a large jos house stands fronting an avenue of colossal granite figures of men and animals,

extending in a semicircular sweep for about a
mile, to two square, brick, Egyptian-shaped
buildings, which are hollow, open on each side,
and empty.   These, we were told, were the
tombs of the emperors of the Ming dynasty ; but
our guide also said, that there was a large excavation in the rock behind the jos house containing coffins ; so I fancy that it must be the
place of general interment, and that the huge
figures were merely intended to dignify the
approach to the cemetery.   We had not time to
visit the jos house, but we trotted our startled
horses between these silent guards, and examined
with great interest the sculpture of a departed
age — they are about three times the size of life.
A tablet gate marks the commencement of the
avenue ; then in succession appear two upright
shafts of granite in single blocks, four warriors
dressed in long loose shirts of scale armour,
leaning with folded hands upon their swords,
(they front each other, as do all the statues,) next
to them, lions, bears, horses, camels, elephants,
and so on to the two buildings, a repetition of
the same figures, each alternate pair (with the
exception of the men) crouching.   Most of them
have been hewn into shape from single blocks :
they rest upon flat slabs of granite, on un-
levelled ground, and, strange to say, although
centuries have passed since they were first placed

there, no weeds are growing around, nor have they sunk three inches.

The elephants are accurately shaped, and fairly sculptured; the rest are all most rudely executed.

We rode close under a portion of the old wall, which we computed to be seventy feet in height: three sides are protected by the deep broad canal; the fourth and eastern by stagnant ponds opposite the points most accessible.

We passed through several villages, all with their shops open and filled with staring crowds. We took them by surprise; and the loud babble which we had heard at a considerable distance hushed, on our appearance, into perfect silence : every occupation was instantly suspended, and every eye in the thronged streets turned upon us in grave wonderment and apprehension.

We crossed the canal twice over low stone bridges. Two of the city gates were open close to where we passed, and from them, as the rapid intelligence of our approach spread, issued thousands: they pressed upon our rear, and blocked by numbers every lane and avenue, but left our front entirely open.

We had seen the pagoda over the S.W. angle of the city wall for some miles before we turned

I 6

the corner: when this point was passed, it stood
forth to our view, uninterrupted from ball to base
by a single intervening object: it more than
realised our expectations.

It is an octagonal building of nine stories, rising
to the height of 261 feet; bright with many-
coloured porcelain, which throws off a glittering
light like the reflected rays from gems: it is in
perfect preservation.

The porcelain is fastened to the tower with
mortar, as Dutch tiles are upon a stove, except the projecting cornices and bas reliefs of
grotesque monsters, which are nailed.   The
various colours are white, yellow, red, and green;
the roofing tiles are all of the imperial yellow.

It stands in a spacious court, surrounded on
three sides by a wall, the fourth open to two
extensive flights of granite steps descending to
the jos house attached to the pagoda facing the
town.   Another large enclosure planted with
 egular rows of trees extends to the road and
suburbs.

The projecting flanges, if I may so term them,
of the separate stories curve upwards at the
points, to which are suspended bells of size pro-
portioned to the taper of the tower.   A priest
assured me that when they were first hung up,
after the complete repair of the paoută, or pagoda,

in the last century, they used to ring forth
charming melodies at the command of the mistress
of the tower, " the Queen of Heaven," until she,
wrathful at the indifference and falling off of
her followers, in a fit of anger, deprived them
of sound.   The greater portion are certainly
tongueless, and all of them cracked, which is
not surprising, for the bells and cast gongs in
China (made of the same metal) are very brittle,
from the absence of an adequate proportion of
alloy.

After we had tethered our horses in the court-
yard, away from the immense and momentarily
increasing crowd, we entered the pagoda by the
principal door in front of the flight of steps,
and found ourselves in an extensive octagonal
corridor surrounding the body of the building,
which is square and elaborately ornamented with
figures of the Budha faith in bas relief — the
whole profusely gilt : each story contained a
shrine with the universal idol, the sitting figure
of " the Queen of Heaven."

A single door under the niche, in which the
principal deity was placed, leads into a square
chamber in the shaft of the building, occupied by
another image.   The walls are all lined with
square porcelain tiles, each separate one embossed with a small device in the centre : those

upon the ground-floor are entirely covered with gilding. The others of the eight upper stories differ, by having a black edging round the gilded device, which has a good effect: the concluding step of each story is of stone, the flooring and stairs of wood.

The ample view from the summit surpassed our expectations. Facing the south, a little river from the distant hills came winding like the Forth near Stirling: it passes by the south and western walls, and helps to supply the canal with water. Towards the S. W., as far as the sight could reach, flowed the princely Yang-tze-kiang, leaving between us and it, as it passed Nanking, a richly cultivated flat of paddy land about three miles in breadth. Facing the north, we looked down upon the walls and roofs of a dense cluster of houses — the Chinese city; through the centre eastward, ran a canal. The streets seemed very narrow; the buildings principally of two low stories; and upon every slight rise of ground public temples, granaries, and government offices, surrounded by spacious yards or courts, were discernible.

Half way between the pagoda and extreme eastern wall the town is bounded by trees and gardens, fields, woods, and grassy plains, over which are scattered a few large public buildings: this scenery extends to a belt of wood which

screens the north and eastern wall from view.
Further to the right the features of the scenery
are slightly altered by the inner wall of the
Tartar city, within which little can be seen for
dense foliage ; and the distance being greater, we
saw less of it from our present stand than from
the hill in the morning.   From that point we
plainly saw the site of the ancient palace and
gardens inhabited by the race of Ming, the citadel,
assembly house, and esplanade of the present
garrison.

The walls are built of brick, of an average
thickness of 25 feet at the top, and 60 at the
bottom, and vary from 35 to 90 in height.   In
places they are built against the escarped sides of
hills, where they cross the even ground and over
the dips : they are as high inside as on the out ;
this we could distinctly see from our position.
They are built, like those at Chin-kiang-foo, of
brick, propped by earthen banks.   Round their
whole extent tents were pitched ; and where the
natural defences were not so good, and opposite
the gates, these were very numerous.   From our
position we looked down upon a guard-house full
of troops, all staring up at us ; their gingals,
matchlocks, bows and arrows, and quick-lime,
were piled in readiness under cover of a shed.
When we first appeared, the soldiers clustered

round their arms, and seemed to meditate revenge for former defeats.   We mustered amongst our party two swords and a pistol, besides the knives and forks.

The present walls of Nanking encircle an undulating plain, and are bounded on three sides by hills of irregular height, and on the fourth by the river.   They form an irregular pentagon : the old walls extend far beyond the present range; they can be traced but with difficulty; and it is asserted that they passed for fifty miles over hill and dale. The new ones, by our rough calculation, measure 22 miles, and have nine gates; seven into the Chinese, two into the Tartar city.

On the top of the highest pagoda in China we drank the health of our Queen in champagne, which our coolies had brought with other good things from the camp.   Our tiffin was cooked on the green under the gaze of many thousands. The foremost ranks of the crowd at one time became so curious to examine the contents of the pots and pans that our fellows had to use rope's ends to save us the pain of fasting.   To my great astonishment they bore the blows most good-humouredly, and afterwards kept a more respectful distance.

During our meal the chief priest came to see us.   His high and narrow forehead, straight nose, and well-formed mouth, showed no indication of Tartar blood. His head was closely shaven, and he wore a long full gown of black silk. His manner was good, and his demeanour modest : he welcomed us to his temple, drank our healths in our own wine, and was greatly taken with two empty beer bottles, which we made him a present of. In exchange, we procured some impressions of the pagoda upon thin paper, with a history attached in Chinese, of which I give a translation in the Appendix.

We rode back the way we came, attended through the suburbs by an immense, but silent, crowd : sulky faces there were in abundance, but none gave vent by expression or gesture to their bitter feelings.

As we repassed the colossal figures before the tombs of the ancient dynasty of Ming the declining sun shed a golden light upon the summits of Chung-shan. A bank of copsewood darkened the breast of the mountain, and threw out in fine relief the yellow tints of the parched plain upon which the grey granite figures stood. It was impossible, while gazing upon the memorials of a royal and by-gone race in the heart of the empire which once they governed, not to feel the scene most forcibly.

The prospect itself was very fine ; and in the

uncertain light of the evening impressed me with mingled emotions of grandeur and of beauty. The colours, tints, regularity, and fine, yet subdued, proportions, of the landscape, and the huge monuments of art, were beautifully blended, and at the hour the whole wore an appearance almost of sublimity — the grand repose of Michael Angelo combined with (in faultless nature) the gentle softness of Raphael.

We arrived at camp after dark, and sufficiently tired to defy a legion of mosquitoes eagerly awaiting our resignation to the arms of Morpheus.

The naval portion of the party returned to the ships early on the 29th, to be in time to see the Commissioners sign the treaty on board the Cornwallis. On my way I called on board the Queen, and saw the Emperor's letters, which had arrived the evening before, assenting (with the exception of free trade with Foo-choo-foo, and which Sir Henry overruled) to all the articles in the rough draft which had been forwarded for his inspection. Although there were perhaps a few objectionable expressions, showing that the leaven of ancient arrogance was not extinct, it nevertheless, from the first word to the last, evinced deep consciousness of fallen power.

Ke-ying and New-king came on board about eleven o'clock in the Admiral's barge; Elipoo

followed in a large boat of his own.   The poor
old man was much debilitated in consequence of
the mandarin who was sent to the Queen for
the medicines having got very drunk and lost the
prescription.   Afraid to confess his delinquency,
he told Elipoo he was to take all the pills and
liquids at once : the result was very apparent ;
he had to be carried into the cabin, and recline
upon a sofa during the whole interview.   He
thanked the doctor for his treatment, and trusted
that the cure would be as certain as the remedy
was violent.

The Commissioners were received with all due
honours ; but our officers were ordered to put on
their undress uniform, in consequence of the Chinese having appeared on both previous occasions
in their ordinary robes.

There were four copies of the treaty written in
both languages, under separate covers : the ends
of the riband which tied them together were
sealed to the paper ; so that, without cutting it,
no sheet could be abstracted — not an unlikely
thing to be attempted by these slippery gentlemen
to blind the eyes of their Imperial master.

From a square box covered with yellow silk
the Treasurer Whang took his writing-pencils,
ink, and the official seal of the Viceroy : it was
an agate about three and a half inches long by

two broad: this was pressed against a pad saturated with red lead, and then applied to the paper. The three Commissioners signed their names under the impression, and thus ratified the Plenipotentiary's first and last demands.

It was a glorious spectacle for all who saw it. Two hundred miles within their greatest river, under the walls of their ancient capital, in the cabin of a British 74, the first treaty China was ever forced to make was signed by three of her highest nobles under England's flag.

After this they entered the fore-cabin to take refreshments. The Admiral gave the health of their Majesties, the Queen of Great Britain and the Emperor of China; upon which a royal salute was fired.

They went away at last, doubtless with humble pride, but just satisfaction at having saved their ancient city, and perhaps their monarch's throne; but long will it be, if ever, before his complete supremacy will again be felt; long will it be before the lament of the fatherless, the anarchy and starvation, or the misery of the houseless wanderers over the richest portion of his vast empire, will be a forgotten tale.

CHAP. XIII.

THE IMPERIAL COMMISSIONERS, KE-YING, ELIPOO, AND NEW-KING. — DEPARTURE FROM NANKING. — GREAT SIZE OF YANG-TZE-KIANG.

THE mandarins who were so intimately connected with us during the latter period of my stay with the expedition deserve a more detailed notice than has hitherto been bestowed upon them; and although my information may, in some minor points, be incorrect, I can vouch for the general accuracy of the slight sketches I shall give of the three principal men.

Ke-ying or Kih-ying, the chief Commissioner, well deserves the gratitude of his country and kindly feeling and respect from us.

A Manchow Tartar of the Imperial kindred, born near the northern frontier of the empire, his profession from youth upwards has been one of arms : in it he rose by bravery and conduct to be generalissimo of the Tartar army. This post with those of Tsung-shin (viceroy) of the province of Kirin, and Se-ang-keun (guardian of the heir apparent), confined him to the court and frontiers, so that he never had an opportunity of joining in warfare against us, or doing aught besides tendering his counsel, and arranging the necessary supplies and reinforcements.

But at last, plainly perceiving that a true, ungarbled statement of the direful losses of the Chinese had never reached the Imperial ear, he determined to quit his high appointments and repair to the scene of action, to see and faithfully report thereon at every risk.

I believe he reached the province of Kiang-su shortly after Chin-kiang-foo was taken. He had prepared himself to expect a partial stoppage of internal commerce, a stagnation of trade, a certain depression of spirits, and a loss of self-confidence from constant defeat; but he never contemplated the utter paralysation of all energy, the apathetic torpor which had succeeded the first paroxysm of fear and despair, that he met with among the multitudes unhoused both by us and the native banditti. He did not fail to perceive that the principal danger to be apprehended by his countrymen, if the war should continue, was from their own rabble, who had availed themselves of the interruption of all constituted authority, caused by our successes, to assemble from every direction, to enter cities, throw open state prisons, plunder the treasuries, destroy the granaries, and commit every enormity. He

saw that unless a speedy peace was concluded the
fall of Nanking would be inevitable, and that the
safety of the empire itself would become precarious.
He thus felt the full necessity of showing his Imperial master the danger in its gloomiest colours,
knowing that until he viewed it thus he never
would agree to do what he considered the deepest
degradation — sue for peace.   Ke-ying also knew
the great risk that he himself would incur by being
the first man to hazard a narration of the truth,
but this did not deter him : — he informed the
Emperor of all that had been before concealed from
him — of what they had to expect from a continued resistance, and transmitted a faithful copy
of our demands, including a clear and capital letter
from Sir Henry Pottinger, in answer to one from
himself sent to Chin-kiang-foo, requesting an interview.

Fortunately for his head and the lives of thousands, the Emperor was convinced, and by return
of courier he received full powers to associate
himself with Elipoo.

His age may be between sixty and seventy : he
is a stout, hale, good-humoured-looking old gentleman with a firm step, and upright carriage. At
first we were prejudiced against his intellectual
endowments, but when business commenced, he
threw off his apparent dulness, and became all

animation, and evinced considerable shrewdness and observation.

He wore a dark silk dress without embroidery, girded by a yellow belt, the indication of his high birth, and a summer cap with a red opaque ball and peacock's feather.

He was vested with the rank of Imperial Commissioner, with plenary powers : — Kin-chai-peen e ping sze ta chin — literally, *"imperially appointed, convenient, proper to act business, great minister."*

If Ke-ying deserves the lasting gratitude of his country, poor old Elipoo has an equal right to ours, as the preserver of the lives of Major Anstruther and others of our countrymen, at the risk of his own popularity, besides his unvarying kindness and care for all the prisoners who fell into his hands, which humanity eventually excited the suspicions of his master, who in consequence deprived him of the government of the province of Tseen-ko.

Amiable as wise, he was one of those high officers who inclined to the pacific counsels of Ke-shan ; and knowing what misery a war would entail, was willing to trust to the equity of our first demands rather than hazard an accumulation of evils and ill feeling, without a prospect of gaining any satisfactory result, knowing that the evil which they fought with one hand to expel was grasped with greater tenacity by the other.

Elipoo is a Tartar of the Imperial clan Hong-
tai-tze, literally "red girdle," a mandarin of the
first rank and button, Taon-yih-ping-tang-tai,
entitled to wear the peacock's feather Nwa-ling *,
a lieutenant-general of Chapoo, previously a viceroy, Tseen-ko-tŭh-foo-tang — member of the
privy council, Nuy-ko-chung-tang.

New-king is a man who from his youth upwards
has been devoted to self-indulgence : at one period
to such an extent of extravagance did his habits
carry him, that his emoluments and large fortune
were completely absorbed, and he was, it is said,
reduced to a state of beggary.   Under these circumstances he had recourse (while any stock in
hand lasted) to the pawn shop, until he was in
the condition of Chaucer's knight —

> " All his means of living gone,
> Ermine, mantle had he none ;
> And in pawn had long been laid,
> Cap and mantle of brocade ;
> Harness rich, and charger stout,
> All were eat and drunken out."

In this state, while his coffers required no lock
and key, some unforeseen good fortune, the origin of which my informant was not able clearly
to explain, brought him again into notice, and

---

* This decoration was worn by Elipoo, Ke-ying, and
New-king, as well as by Whang, the treasurer, the Tartar
General, and Chun, prefect of Ning-po.

he now is president of the board of war, Ning-foo-shang-shoo ; viceroy of the provinces of Keang-nan and Keang-see, Leang-keang-toung-tŭh-foo-tang ; and was beaten by us while in command of the Imperial troops at Woo-sung ; from the field of which really well-fought battle he affirms he was borne away in the arms of his faithful attendants, in spite of his earnest remonstrances.

He is certainly the least intellectual looking of the three, has an elongated face with swollen lower eye-lids, colourless, unfirm flesh, and hanging cheeks — his whole appearance strongly indicative of his mode of life. He wore the same dress and button as the other two, with the exception of the red and yellow girdles.

Whang, the treasurer, is the person whom I have mentioned before as having been sent by the Commissioners to negotiate the preliminary arrangement of the treaty : he is considered one of the most rising young men in China. He wore a blue ball and peacock's feather.

Chun, prefect of Ning-po, is the officer who planned and attempted the destruction of our garrison at that place. He attacked us during the night, and was repulsed with great slaughter.

He was very kind to Major Anstruther during his imprisonment, and has the reputation of being an able magistrate ; he also was decorated with the peacock's feather, and wore a white crystal button over the usual red tassel, made from the hair of the *yack*, or grunting ox (the hair from the tail of this animal is also much used for pennons to their spears and banners).

After the treaty was signed the Plenipotentiary permitted travellers to cross the river, but the blockade was to continue until the first instalment was paid.

Boats full of fruit, vegetables, china ware, and visiters flocked alongside the nearest ships, and comparative animation was restored to the scene.

On the 31st of August, 1842, I wished my kind and gallant Commander-in-chief, Sir William Parker, good-by, and embarked on board the H. C. S. Tanasserim, and commenced the descent of the magnificent river.

I cannot bid farewell to it without attempting to do it justice by placing it in its proper position, as one of the largest rivers of the first class.

It is believed by some of our best geographers, that in consequence of its source issuing from mountains, and its course traversing countries outside the tropics, away from the influence of the regions of rain, which lie under the equator, its volume cannot be in proportion to its great length, as the waters from the melting of the snow and periodical rains never accumulate into such a body as those fed by the tropical rains.

This admitted hypothesis renders the great size of the Yang-tze-kiang still more extraordinary, presenting by our casual measurement of depth, breadth, and rapidity of current, a volume of water second only to the Amazon and the Orinoko. This fact may, upon farther examination, be found to arise from some great tributary coming from the S. W.

At the mouth the Yang-tze-kiang is inferior, both in breadth and depth, to several streams of a less actual magnitude. Its estuary measures about sixty miles, and the average depth over the mud bar is scarce six fathoms. But yet eighty miles higher up, a body of water, eight miles broad, and sixty feet deep, rolls towards the ocean at the rate of five miles an hour: 200 miles from the sea, off the walls of Nanking, the breadth is 3600 feet, with an equal depth of twenty-two fathoms from within fifty paces of the northern shore to the rushes on the southern.

The Amazon, rising from among the western mountains on the broad shoulder of South America, receives the tribute of all the streams as it descends in a parallel latitude towards the Atlantic: it is the drain to the lower lands, saturated by, perhaps, the heaviest and most continued rain in the universe; in shape, like a huge pine, its expansive mouth is in itself a sea, and throws forth its waters unmixed for miles into the ocean.

The Cambajor and Irrawaddy, although of greater length, have less magnitude of waters than the Ganges, the Indus, or the Brahmaputra, which are fed by the rains drawn down from the humid clouds of the ocean, carried by the S. W. monsoon over the peninsula of Hindostan.

So we find this Chinese river, of the first magnitude, the exception to the rule.

The Yang-tze-kiang (as far as we have ascertained) free for 2000 miles of broken and abrupt descents, uninterrupted by impediments, unfiltered for 3000 miles by any dividing branch, pours on through peopled countries, filling streams so numerous that they and their inland contributions are the high roads supplied by nature — the ways of transport for surrounding millions. Within 150 miles from its mouth, the artificial banks alone protect the flat alluvial country from inundation. Sluices and canals drain off the river water for many miles for the purposes of agriculture. The porous earth, which for the benefit of the young rice is kept almost continually

flooded, aided by the sun's powerful rays, absorbs
a vast quantity of its waters, and may, I imagine,
be one great cause why the depth at the mouth
does not correspond with the great profundity
and volume to be met with higher up in this
great river.

APPENDIX.

APPENDIX.

IMPERIAL EDICTS.

By a national statute it is required that the sacred edict, containing sixteen maxims written by the Emperor Kang-he, be proclaimed throughout the empire by the local officers on the 1st and 15th of every moon. The manner of doing this is thus described in the under-mentioned authority * : —

"Early on the 1st and 15th of every moon, the civil and military officers, dressed in their uniforms, meet in a clean spacious public hall. The Superintendant, who is called Le-sang, calls aloud, ' Stand forth in files ;' they do so according to their rank : he then says, ' Kneel thrice and bow the head nine times ;' they kneel and bow to the ground with their faces towards a platform, on which is placed a board with the Emperor's name. He then calls aloud, ' Rise and retire ;' they rise and all go to a hall or kind of chapel, where the law (sacred edict) is usually read, and where the military and people are assembled, standing round in silence. The Le-sang then says, ' Respectfully commence ;' the Sze-keang-sang, or orator, advancing towards an incense altar, kneels,

* See *Chinese Repository*, vol. i. p. 299.

reverentially, takes up the board on which the maxim appointed for the day is written, and ascends a stage with it. An old man receives the board and puts it down on the stage fronting the people; then commanding silence with a wooden rattle which he carries in his hand, he kneels and reads it. When he has finished, the Le-sang calls out, " Explain such a maxim or section of the sacred edict.' The orator stands up and gives the sense, namely, rehearses the amplification or paraphrase, or both. We take the sixteen maxims in their order, copying them from the translation : —

" 1. Pay just regard to filial and fraternal duties, in order to give due importance to the relations of life.

" 2. Respect kindred, in order to display the excellence of harmony.

" 3. Let concord abound among those who dwell in the same neighbourhood, in order to prevent litigations.

" 4. Give the chief place to husbandry and the culture of the mulberry tree, in order to procure adequate supplies of food and raiment.

" 5. Hold economy in estimation, in order to prevent the lavish waste of money.

" 6. Magnify academical learning, in order to direct the scholar's progress.

" 7. Degrade strange religions, in order to exalt the orthodox doctrines.

" 8. Explain the laws, in order to warn the ignorant and obstinate.

" 9. Illustrate the principles of a polite and yielding carriage, in order to improve manners.

" 10. Attend to the essential employments, in order

to give unvarying determination to the will of the people.

" 11. Instruct the youth, in order to prevent them from doing evil.

" 12. Suppress all false accusing, in order to secure protection to the innocent.

" 13. Warn those who hide deserters, that they may not be involved in their downfall.

" 14. Complete the payment of taxes, in order to prevent frequent urging.

" 15. Unite the *paon* and *kea**, in order to extirpate robbery and theft.

" 16. Settle animosities, that lives may be duly valued."

PORCELAIN PAGODA.

COMPILED FROM A COLLECTION OF SKETCHES BY KINLUNG, IN WHICH IS A REPRESENTATION OF A TEMPLE DEDICATED TO THE HONOUR OF BUDHA.

" That at as remote a period of the world as the reign of Sun Woo, the great Emperor, this temple was erected, and at successive periods additions and repairs were made from time to time. Originally the temple occupied a small square space of ground called Soo-Leung, but the priest Lew-Lung, O, obtained a grant of land, in extent 1000 le, within which space its limits were to be confined. The Emperor Wan-te, of the Tsin dynasty, having at

---

* Ten families form a *kea*, and ten *keas* constitute a *paon*.

this time made an addition to it, it took the name
of Chang-Tseen-Sze, and during his reign it was
raised to the height of three stories. In the reign
of Kaon-Tsung (or the first emperor), of the Tung
dynasty, extensive repairs were made, and the name
altered to Teen-He-Sze (the temple — the delight of
heaven). In the reign of Kien-Tïh, the founder of
the Sing dynasty, the name was altered to that of
Teze-Gan-Tsung-Chung (the temple conferring fa-
vours, imparting faith and charity). During the reign
of Yung-Lo (eternal joy) the Empress caused to be
commenced the northern wall of the enclosure as an
offering, and the work continued till the 1st day, 8th
moon, 6th year of Seun-Tïh — a period of 19 years.

" The boards of works then caused a detailed
plan of the structure to be printed ; its height being
32 changs *, 9 covids, 4 puntos, and 9-10ths of a
punto, and its roof surmounted by a ball, both of
which were covered with brass plates of an endless
brightness. On the roof of the ninth story project
dragons' heads, in whose mouths are attached ten
chains which ascend to the apex of the roof, each
having 72 links : above and below, at the eight
corners, the chains amount to 80 in number, making
a total of 152 ; while on the outside of the nine stories
there are stands or supports for 128 lamps ; within,
each chamber, and also the centre of the roof, are supplied with glazed horn lanterns ; the quantity of oil
required to fill them being 64 catties (81 lbs.), and the
brilliant appearance they create ascends to the heavens.
The apex is surmounted by a copper ball, whose

* A chang is thirteen feet.

weight is 900 catties (1200 lbs.): it contains a dish
for sacrifice, and it is of the weight of 450 catties
(600 lbs.). From the east, looking towards the sea;
from the south, where is the garden of the Tung-Foo;
towards the west, where is the bridge called the Le-
pin; and towards the north, where is the great river
(Yang-tze-kiang), the distance is 9 le, 13 poos (about
$2\frac{1}{2}$ miles).

" From the reign of Yung-Lo, when it underwent a
thorough repair, an hundred ages have experienced
its benefits, protection, and favour; it is therefore
called Paon-Gan-Sze (the temple of the protecting
favour). From the first story throughout the building,
the whole cost of labour has amounted to 2,485,484
tales (equal to about $3\frac{1}{2}$ millions of dollars). On the
roof stretching up to the apex are nine iron rings, the
largest of which is 6 changs 3 covids (about 75 feet) in
circumference, and the smallest 2 covids 4 puntos, the
entire weight being 3600 catties (4800 lbs). It has a
beam in the roof which shines during the darkest
night; one that keeps off danger from fire; another
from water; and one that defends it from the violence
of the winds; while a fifth guards against the effects
of earthquakes. In the same place, the roof, there is a
gold rod of the weight of 40 tales, tea leaves one
bushel, silver 1000 tales, a mirror weighing 100
catties, a gem of great value, cash of the reign of
Yung-Lo, 1000 strings, silk of the Imperial yellow two
pieces, one collection of the chemical works of the
king, or holy book of Fo, one copy, and two or three
treating of the religion of Budha;—all these relics
are in the roof.

" Now in the 5th year of the reign of Kea-king,

during the 5th moon, 15th day, the God of Thunder caused it to be injured in three places, and at the same time the whole of the nine stories received damage. Really was the strength of the gods manifested with fearful awe and severity : the idols (not being susceptible to injury from causes which affect material objects) were untouched.

" The governor and Foo-Yeun (deputy-governor) then in a clear and luminous communication represented to the throne the extent of the disasters, and solicited workmen to repair it. In the 7th year of Kea-king, 2d moon, 6th day, they commenced, and having thoroughly repaired and beautified the temple, they ceased work on the 2d day of the 6th moon, since when it has undergone no change."

TREATY OF PEACE

CONCLUDED BETWEEN ENGLAND AND CHINA.

The following are the most important provisions :—

1. Lasting peace and friendship between the two empires.

2. China to pay twenty-one millions of dollars in the course of the present and three succeeding years.

3. The ports of Canton, Amoy, Foo-choo-foo, Ningpo, and Shang-hai, to be thrown open to British merchants; consular officers to be appointed to reside at them, and regular and just tariffs of import and export (as well as inland transit) duties to be established and published.

4. The island of Hong-Kong to be ceded in perpetuity to her Britannic Majesty, her heirs and successors.

5. All subjects of her Britannic Majesty (whether natives of Europe or India) who may be confined in any part of the Chinese empire to be unconditionally released.

6. An act of full and entire amnesty to be published by the Emperor, under his Imperial sign-manual and seal, to all Chinese subjects, on account of their having held service, or intercourse with, or resided under the British government, or its officers.

7. Correspondence to be conducted on terms of perfect equality amongst the officers of both governments.

8. On the Emperor's assent being received to this treaty, and the payment of the first six million dollars, her Britannic Majesty's forces to retire from Nanking and the Grand Canal, and the military posts at Ting-hae to be also withdrawn; but the islands of Chusan and Kolongsoo are to be held until the money payments and the arrangements for opening the ports be completed.

Dated on board her Majesty's ship Cornwallis, in the Yang-tze-kiang river, off Nanking, this 30th day of August, 1842.

(Signed)   HENRY POTTINGER,
Her Majesty's Plenipotentiary.

(A true copy.)   G. A. MALCOLM,
Secretary of Legation.

TOPOGRAPHY OF KIÁNGSÚ. *

BOUNDARIES AND SITUATION OF THE PROVINCE; ITS
AREA AND POPULATION; DEPARTMENTS AND DIS-
TRICTS; RIVERS, LAKES, MOUNTAINS, PRODUCTIONS,
ETC.

FORMERLY, and until the peaceful and prosperous
times of the present dynasty, the provinces of Kiángsú
and A'nhwui were united in one, under the name of
Kiángnán; so they are described by Du Halde, and
often so spoken of at the present day. Thus, the
government of the Liáng Kiáng includes, together
with these two provinces, that of Kiángsí. The province is bounded on the north by Shántung; on the
east by the sea; on the south by Chekiáng; and on
the west by A'nhwui and Hònán. Its shape, on
native maps, is rhomboidal, with the longest sides
running from the north-west to the south-east, and the
shortest from east to west. The extreme north is in
lat. 35° 10′, and the southern limit in lat. 31° 20′,
giving an extent of 3° 50′ from north to south; in
longitude it extends from 5′ to 5° 5′ east from Peking.
Of the line of coast little is known, except that it is
studded with the low islands and sand banks, evidently formed by the disemboguement of the two
great rivers, the Yángtsz'kiáng and the Yellow River.
Commencing at the north-east on the sea, following
closely the line of demarcation, you run first north-
west, then west, and round the south, crossing and
twice recrossing the river Mu; thence due west across

* From the *Chinese Repository*, April, 1842.

seven small streams, and then turning short to the
south you run down to and over the Grand canal;
going on a little to the south, you then turn to the
north-west, and sweep around to the south-west, to the
Yellow River. Thus far you have Shántung on one
side of the line. On the south of this river, for a
short distance, perhaps fifty miles, the province borders
on Hònán, and the line runs from the north-west to
the south-east. It now separates this province from
that of A'nhwui, and runs first east, then south, and
again east, or rather south-east; and in this direction
it continues on to the sea, dividing Kiángsú from
Chekiáng.

Its area must be nearly that of Chekiáng, which has
been estimated to contain 39,150 square miles, making
25,056,000 English acres. The population is much
larger than that of Chekiáng, being put down at
37,843,501 souls.

Kiángsú is divided into twelve departments, and
sixty-seven districts — it having 8 fú, 1 chilí ting, and
3 chilí chau, with 2 ting, 3 chau, and 62 hien — the
names of which are as follows, taken from the imperial
authority.

I. *Kiángning fú*, or the department of Kiángning,
includes seven districts. Its chief city is situated in
lat. 32° 4′ 30″ N., and long. 2° 18′ 34″ E. of Peking,
and 118° 43′ 34″ E. of Greenwich.

1. Shángyuen,	5. Kiángpú,
2. Kiángning,	6. Lishui,
3. Káushun,	7. Luho.
4. Küyung,	

II. *Súchau fú*, or the department of Súchau, includes ten districts. Its chief city is situated in lat.

31° 23′ 25″ N., long. 4° 0′ 25″ E. of Peking, and 120° 25′ 25″ E. of Greenwich.

1. Wú *hien,*	6. Chángshu,
2. Chángchau,	7. Cháuwan,
3. Yuenhò,	8. Kwanshán,
4. Wúkiáng,	9. Sinyáng,
5. Chintse,	10. Táihú *ting.*

III. *Sungkiáng fú,* or the department of Sung-kiáng, includes eight districts. Its chief city is situated in lat. 30° N., and long. 4° 28′ 34″ E. of Peking, and 120° 53′ 34″ E. of Greenwich.

1. Hwáting,	5. Kinshán,
2. Lau *hien,*	6. Shánghái,
3. Nánhwái,	7. Chuenshá *ting,*
4. Funghien,	8. Tsingpú.

IV. *Chángchau fú,* or the department of Cháng-chau, includes eight districts. Its chief city is situated in lat. 31° 50′ 36″ N., long. 3° 24′ 17″ E. of Peking, and 119° 49′ 17″ E. of Greenwich.

1. Yánghú,	5. Kinkwei,
2. Wútsin,	6. Wúyáng,
3. I'hing,	7. Kiángyin,
4. Kingkí,	8. Tsingkiáng.

V. *Chingkiáng fú,* or the department of Chinkiáng, includes four districts. Its chief city is situated in lat. 32° 14′ 26″ N., long. 2° 55′ 43″ E. of Peking, and 119° 20′ 43″ E. of Greenwich.

1. Tántú,	3. Kintán,
2. Tányáng,	4. Liyáng.

VI. *Hwái'án, fú,* or the department of Hwái'án, includes six districts. Its chief city is situated in lat.

33° 32′ 24″ N., long. 2° 45′ 42″ E. of Peking, and 119° 10′ 42″ E. of Greenwich.

1. Shányáng,	4. A′ntung,
2. Yenching,	5. Tsinghò,
3. Fauning,	6. Táuyuen.

VII. *Yángchau fú,* or the department of Yáng-chau, includes eight districts. Its chief city is situated in lat. 32° 26′ 32″ N., long. 2° 55′ 43″ E. of Peking, and 119° 20′ 43″ E. of Greenwich.

1. Kiángtú,	5. Páuying,
2. Kántsiuen,	6. Hinghwá,
3. I′ching,	7. Tungtái,
4. Káuyú *chau,*	8. Tái *chau.*

VIII. *Süchau fú,* or the department of Süchau, includes eight districts. Its chief city is situated in lat. 34° 15′ 8″ N., and long. 0° 57′ E. of Peking.

1. Tungshán,	5. Yángshán,
2. Shuining,	6. Fung *hien,*
3. Sutsien,	7. Pei *hien,*
4. Siáu *hien,*	8. Pei *chau.*

IX. *Háimun ting,* or the department of Háimun. has only one district,

Háimun.

X. *Hái chau,* or the department of Hái, includes two districts. Its chief city is situated in lat. 34° 32′ 24″ N., and long. 2° 55′ 47″ E. of Peking.

1. Muyang,	2. Hányü.

XI. *Tung chau,* or the department of Tung, includes two districts. Its chief city is situated in lat. 32° 3′ 40″ N., and long. 4° 12′ 42″ E. of Peking, and 120° 37′ 42″ E. of Greenwich.

1. Jükáu,	2. Táihing.

XII. *Táitsáng chau,* or the department of Táitsáng, includes four districts.

1. Chinyáng,   3. Páushán,
2. Kiáting,   4. Tsungming.

The latitude and longitude of some of the chief towns of this province have not been ascertained, or, at least, have not been given by any Europeans. However, they are marked on the Chinese maps with sufficient clearness to enable us to describe their positions accurately enough for the general reader.

1. *The department of Kiángning* includes the ancient Nánking, or the Southern capital — once the most celebrated city of China, whether regard be had to its extent, its buildings, its manufactures, or the character of its inhabitants. The department comprises seven districts ; two of them, Shángyuen and Kiángning, have the residences of their chief magistrates in the provincial capital : Küyung, the chief town of the district of the same name, and the residence of its chief magistrate, is situated on the east of the department ; Líshui and Káushun are on the south ; Kiángpú is on the west ; and Luhó is on the north. This department forms the south-west portion of the province ; on the north and north-east it is bounded by the department of Yángchau ; on the east by that of Chinkiáng ; and on the west and south by the province of A'nhwui. Its greatest extent is from north to south. The Yángstz' kiáng flows through it, so dividing it that about one third of its area is on the northern, and the rest of the department on the southern bank of that majestic river.

The members of Lord Amherst's embassy are, we

believe, the only foreigners who have visited Nánking in modern times; and it is from their writings that we select most of the few particulars which we have to give regarding that city. It stands on the southern bank of the river, and distant from it about three miles. Several canals lead from the river to the city, and also one road, on which some of the members of the embassy walked to the northern gate : this gate is a simple archway, thirty-five paces broad, the height of the wall forty feet, and its width seventeen. Mr. Ellis, and three of the other gentlemen of the embassy, succeeded in passing completely through the uninhabited part of the city, which at present seems to comprise much more than half of the whole area within the walls. The outline of the city, as marked by the walls, is very irregular, approaching to a right-angled triangle, the southern wall being the base, and the western the perpendicular, nearly twice the length of the base. Mr. Ellis and his friends visited one of the vapour-baths, " where," he says, " dirty Chinese may be stewed clean for ten *tsien*, or three farthings each : the bath is a small room of one hundred feet area, divided into compartments, and paved with coarse marble : the heat is considerable; and as the number admitted into the bath has no limits but the capacity of the area, the stench is excessive." Another gentleman of the embassy, Mr. Poole, says the outermost of the three compartments was lined with closets for the reception of the clothes of bathers, who undressed in this division of the establishment. The closets were all ticketed. One was called the bath of fragrant waters. The two other divisions of the buildings were beyond the first : the largest, on the right hand, containing three baths, about six feet in length, and three in width and depth. " At the time of our visit they were filled with Chinese, rather washing than bathing themselves, who stood upright in the water, which was only a few inches deep, and threw it by turns over each other's backs. There appeared no intention of renewing the water, thus become saturated with dirt, for the use of many other Chinese who waited their turn in the outer apartment. The steam arising from it, however fragrant to the senses of the Chinese, was to mine really intolerable, and drove me away before I could ascertain in what manner the baths were heated. I just looked into the adjoining room, and found it furnished with matted benches, and that it was used by the bathers to dry themselves in before going to dress in the outer apartment." The walls of Nánking, judging from a specimen carried away by Abel, are built of grey compact limestone, which he says frequently occurs in quarries in its neighbourhood. Mr. Davis speaks of a striking resemblance between the city of Nánking, with the area within the walls but partially inhabited, and ruins of buildings lying here and there, and that of Rome. Le Comte's account of the Porcelain pagoda may be found in the first volume of the *Chinese Repository*, p. 257.

II. *The department of Súchau* is nearly square ; it lies on the south of the Great River, and extends southward from it to the province of Chekiáng, having the departments of Táitsáng and Sungkiáng on the east, and that of Chángchau on the west. The magistrates of three districts have their residences at Súchau : these districts are, Chángchau on the east, Yuenhò on the west, and Wúhien in the middle between the two. From Súchau, the chief town of the department, the districts of Kwanshán and Sinyáng lie on the east, their chief magistrates both (judging from the map) residing in one city; the districts of Wúkiáng and Chintse lie on the south, their magistrates likewise both dwelling within the same walls; the district of Táihú is situated on an island in the Great Lake, and hence its name (Táihú *ting*); the remaining two districts, Chángshu and Cháuwan, are situated on the north of the department, their chief magistrates residing in one and the same city, near the "Great River,"— as the Yángtsz' kiáng is emphatically and very commonly called.

" Above," say the Chinese, " there is paradise (or the palace of heaven) — below are Sú and Háng;" *i. e.* the cities of Súchau and Hángchau. All that was said, in the last number, in praise of Hángchau, may be said, with equal propriety, of Súchau. We subjoin, however, some additional particulars, collected from one of the histories of the department : the work is called " Súchau fú Chí," and is comprised in forty octavo volumes, making eighty-two chapters, besides long and laboured introductions.

Among the remarkable things noticed in these introductions are the *siun hing*, or "imperial visits,"— if we may translate the phrase by giving its equivalent, instead of the literal sense of the two words : *siun* means to go round, as a circuit judge, and as the emperor used to do on tours of inspection ; *hing* means to bless, as the emperor does any and all places that he visits. Kánghí twice visited Súchau ; once in the

23rd year of his reign, and again in the 28th. Kien-lung also visited the city repeatedly.

Chapter 1st comprises several maps, showing the shape of Súchau, the city, and the whole department, with all its districts and principal rivers and lakes : it also contains *kú kin yuen ke piáu,* — a list of all the ancient and modern names which the place has had at different times ; with *yuen ke cháng tsie,* — minute and clear explanations of the reasons for these changes. Its most ancient name was *Yángchau,* and it was then without the pale of civilisation ; subsequently it was called Wú. This name it bore in the times of the Three Kingdoms.

Chapter 2nd comprises two topics : the first is *fan yé sing kwei ;* the second is *tsiáng í.* The phrase *fan yé sing kwei* has reference to that part of the heavens under which the place is situated, and its bearing in regard to the sun and other celestial bodies. Under the second phrase, *tsiáng í,* are noticed in chronological order all the strange and ominous occurrences that have happened at Súchau — such as eclipses, falling stars, appearances of comets, earthquakes, famines, plagues, locusts, inundations, hurricanes, remarkable births, talking dogs, strange sights, miraculous events, fruitful seasons, droughts, running and falling of mountains, square eggs producing a monkey, &c.

Chapter 3rd gives the *kiáng yi,* and *hing shing,* shape of the department.

Chapter 4th details the particulars of the *ching chí,* cities and moats, giving their dimensions, gates, &c.

Chapter 5th enumerates and describes, first, the *kún chú,* governmental offices ; and then the *tsáng yi,* granaries, and governmental post-office or caravan-saries.

Chapter 6th describes the *hiáng tú,* large and small villages ; and the *shí chin,* markets, marts, &c.

Chapter 7th enumerates the *fáng hiáng,* streets, lanes, of various sorts and dimensions.

Chapter 8th gives the names of all the *kiáu liáng,* bridges ; and *kwán tsin,* passes.

Chapter 9th gives the names of the *shán fau,* hills and mountains.

Chapter 10th describes the *shúi táu,* water courses, such as lakes, rivers, canals, &c.

Chapter 11th is occupied with the *hò hing,* or form of the rivers, giving their dimensions, &c.

Chapters 12th to 15th are occupied with the *shúi lí,* or water privileges.

Chapters 16th to 19th contain lists of the *chi kún,* office-bearers, through all the successive dynasties.

Chapter 20th contains the *hú kau,* or censuses, extending from the Chau dynasty downwards.

Chapter 21st relates to the *fung su,* or manners and customs of the people.

Chapter 22d enumerates the *wu chán,* productions of all sorts, animal, vegetable, mineral, and manufactured.

Chapters 23d to 26th relate to the *tien fú,* taxes of various kinds.

Chapter 27th relates to those classes of persons called *yáu yu,* who are employed by the officers of government, as messengers, keepers of prisons.

Chapter 28th describes the institutions of learning, called *hió hiáu,* which terms include colleges, and all the minor schools.

L

Chapters 29th to 34th relate to *suen kü*, the selected and elevated men, who are chosen for high service in the government.

Chapter 36th relates to the military defences, the *ping fáng*, i. e. soldiers, &c.

Chapters 36th and 37th describe the various kinds of sacrificial rites, under the head of *tsz' sz'*.

Chapters 38th to 40th relate to *tsz' khwán*, the religious houses, such as temples, monasteries, &c.

Chapter 41st relates to *tí tse*, the dwellings of the people, describing their situation, &c.

Chapter 42d is filled with notices of the *yuen ting*, gardens, pavilions, arbors, &c.

Chapter 43d contains notices of the *chung mú*, graves, tombs, &c., of distinguished persons.

Chapter 44th relates to *kú tsi*, the antiquities of various kinds, such as monuments, pagodas, and the like.

Chapter 45th contains notices of literary productions, under the head of *i wan*.

Chapters 46th to 53rd are filled with *hwán tsi*, or reminiscences of those who have served the state.

Chapter 54th contains *fung tsió*, or lists of those who have been honoured with titles : it is a chapter on heraldry.

Chapters 55th to 66th contain *lie chuen*, or memoirs of distinguished men.

Chapter 67th contains notices of *háu yiú*, persons distinguished for their filial duty.

Chapter 68th contains notices of *chung í*, or those who have distinguished themselves by loyalty to the state.

Chapters 69th and 70th relate to *wan hió*, the literature and its authors.

Chapter 71st relates to the *wú lió*, or military men, heroes of all ranks.

Chapter 72nd relates to *liú yú*, sojourners and residents, persons who have come from other parts of the empire to reside in this department.

Chapter 73rd relates to *tu hing*, private actions, or notable deeds performed in private life.

Chapter 74th gives notices of *yin yi*, hermits, recluses, &c., who, though possessing ability, chose to live in retirement.

Chapter 75th relates to *hau fi*, queens and imperial ladies of all ranks.

Chapters 76th and 77th notice *lie nü*, eminent women, such as have in any way distinguished themselves by their good conduct.

Chapter 78th relates to the *i shu*, or fine arts, painting, and the like.

Chapter 79th describes the *Shi Táu*, the religious sects of Budha and the Táuists.

The remaining chapters, 80 to 83, are filled with miscellaneous notices, under the head of *tsáh ki*.

This brief outline of the Statistical History of Súchau will afford the reader some idea of the manner in which all things belonging to that department are described. Every province, and almost every department and district in the empire, has its statistical history, in which, as in the one above noticed, a great amount of information is collected and arranged. Volumes of historical, statistical, and descriptive information, regarding Súchau, might be compiled ; but these miscellaneous notices are all that we can now give.

III. *The department of Sungkiáng* comprises eight districts — one *ting* and seven *hien*. It forms the south-east portion of the province, and is of a triangular shape, having Táitsáng chau on the north, the sea on the east and west. The districts Hwáting and Lau *hien* have the residences of their chief magistrates at the city of Sunghiáng. North-east from this city are Shánghái and Chuenshá ; on the east is Nánhwái ; on the south-east is Fung *hien ;* Kinshán is on the south ; and Tsingpú on the north. Shánghái ranks among the largest and richest commercial cities in the empire.

IV. *The department of Chángchau* is of a square form, having Tungchau on the north, Súchau on the east, Chekiáng on the south, and Chinkiáng on the west. Nearly one third of its area is covered with water, the Great River passing through it on the north side, and one half or more of the Great Lake lying within its southern border. The chief magistrates of Yánghú and Wútsin have their residences at Chángchau : north from this city, and on the northern bank of the Great River, is Tsingkiáng ; on the east are Kiángyin, close on the southern bank of the Great River, and Kinkwei and Wúyáng, the chief magistrates of the last two both residing in one and the same city ; on the south are the departments I'hing and Kingkí.

V. *The department of Chinkiáng* is a narrow strip of territory, stretching from the Great River on the north to the province of A'nhwui on the south, having the department of Chángchau on the east, and that of Kiángning on the west. The district of Tántú has the residence of its magistrate at the city of Chinkiáng, close on the southern bank of the Great River ; Tányáng is also not far from the Great River, south-east from Chinkiáng ; Kintán is near the middle of the department; and Líyáng is near the southern border. Du Halde says this department "is one of the most considerable, on account of its situation and trade, being one of the keys of the empire towards the sea, and at the same time a place of defence, where there is a strong garrison."

VI. *The department of Hwái'án* extends from the mouth of the Yellow River, along both its banks, to the western banks of the lake Hungtse. Its chief city "is in imminent danger of being drowned," for the ground on which it stands is lower than the canal, which in several places is supported only by banks of earth : " six miles off," says Du Halde, "it has a borough named Tsingkiáng pú, which is as it were the port of the Yellow River, large and populous; and there resides the surveyor-general of the rivers." The department contains six districts : the magistrate of Tányáng resides at Hwái'án; north from this city is A'ntung; to the north-east from it is Fauning; east is Yenshing; west and north-west are Tsinghó and Tányuen.

VII. *The department of Yángchau* is likewise an extensive region, bounded on the north by Hwái'án, on the east by the sea, on the south by Tungchau and Chinkiáng, on the south-west by Kiángning, and on the west by A'nhwui. It is nearly square in its form, and no inconsiderable portions of its surface are covered with water. It comprises eight districts : two, Kiángtú and Kántsiuen, have the residences of their chief magistrates at Yángchau, which stands not far from the northern bank of the Great River; I'ching stands near it to the south-west; the Great River forms the southern boundary of these three districts. Directly east of

Yángchau is the district of Tái or Tái *chau;* farther towards the north-east is Tungtái. Hinghwá stands in the centre. On the north is Pángying ; and on the west Káuyú *chau:* in this name, and Tái *chau*, the last character or syllable, *chau*, does not constitute a part of the name, but is merely an equivalent for *hien*, a district.

VIII. *The department of Süchau* comprises eight districts, including the whole north-western part of the province, on both sides of the Yellow River, west of the department of Háwi'án. There are four districts on the south side of the river ; Tungshán, the seat of whose chief magistrate is at Süchau, stands midway between the extremes of the department ; north-west from thence is Siáu *hien* and Yángshán ; and in the opposite direction to the south-east is Suining. On the northern side of the river, to the north-west and east, are Peichau and Sutsien.

IX. *The department of Háimun* is geographically described by its name, which, literally translated, means the marine gate, or gate of the sea. It is an island, and stands in the mouth of the Great River, north-west from the greater island of Tsungming.

X. *The department of Hái* is bounded by Shántung on the north and north-west, on the east by the sea, on the south by Hwái'án, and on the west by Süchau. On the west and south-west the river *Mu* forms the boundary of this department, or runs very near it making a right angle at its south-west extreme.

XI. *The department of Tung* is of a triangular shape, situated on the northern bank of the Great River, at its mouth ; so that the sea forms one of its sides, the river another, while the third side is bounded by the department of Yángchau. The chief towns of both of its districts stand some distance removed from the chief town of the department : the latter is on the south, Jükáu is on the west, and Táihing is on the north-west of the department.

XII. *The department of Táitsáng* stands on the southern bank of the Great River, at its mouth, opposite to the department of Tung on the northern bank. It has four districts : Chinyáng on the west ; Kiáting and Páushán on the south and south-west ; and Tsungming stands on an island of the same name ; and it was there that midshipman Hervey was killed, and a site near which he fell is now called Hervey Point. Du Halde, speaking of the island, says that it has three kinds of soil : the first is on the north, wholly uncultivated, and covered only with reeds ; the second extends from the first to the sea on the south, and yields two crops annually ; the third " consists of a greyish sort of earth, dispersed, by spots of the bigness of two acres, over several parts of the island on the north ; it yields so great a quantity of salt, that those of the continent are supplied with it, as well as the islanders. It is pretty difficult to account whence it is that certain portions of land, scattered here and there over the whole country, should be impregnated with salt to such a degree as not to produce a single blade of grass ; while at the same time the lands contiguous to them are very fertile, both in corn and cotton. It often happens also that the fertile lands, in their turn, become salt, and the saline lands fit for sowing."

Probably no territory in the world, of similar extent, is better watered than the province of Kiángsú. The Yángtsz' kiáng, the Yellow River, and the Great Canal, a vast number of lesser streams and branches, with several extensive lakes, afford easy communication by water through almost every part of the whole province. The list of rivers, if made complete, would far exceed that given for Chekiáng. But we shall not, in this article, attempt to give an account of them in detail. The entrance of the Yángtsz' kiáng was quite unknown to European navigators, previously to the surveys which were published in the last volume. We trust that all who may have the means of acquiring additional information, will kindly communicate such for our pages. The embassies of Macartney and Amherst traversed the province, and both on the same course from the frontiers of Shántung to the Great River : there Macartney's turned to the left, and passed on to Hángchau ; while the second turned to the right, and proceeded up the Yángtsz' kiáng. To the several volumes written by the members of those two embassies, our readers are referred for many valuable notices of men and things seen in their journeys.—*Staunton,* vol. ii. p. 398., &c.; *Ellis,* p. 194. ; *Abel,* p. 148. ; and Mr. Davis's new work, noticed in a former number.

There are no mountains, and but few hills, in Kiangsú, the whole province being for the most part one unbroken plain.

The productions are quite the same as those already enumerated as found in Chekiáng, — certainly they are no less in number nor inferior in quality. To Europeans the province presents a rich field for research and observation, regarding the country and its products, the people and their manufactures. Dreadful indeed must be the desolations in this province, if it becomes the theatre of war, as very likely it may in the coming season. Most of its large cities, and they are many, can be approached by small vessels and steamers; whilst vessels of the largest class can, it is believed, move up the Great River quite across the province; and those of the middling class, with the steamers, will probably have no difficulty in reaching the great lake Pòyáng.

CAPTAIN GREY'S OBSERVATIONS.

THE Grand or Imperial Canal has, as far as I could ascertain, three communications with the Yang-tse-keang from the southward. The principal and western-most, after passing under the southern and western walls of Chinkeang-foo, runs through the suburb, and enters the river half a mile below Golden Island; the second is eight miles below, at Santoo, where the canal approaches to within a quarter of a mile of the river; and the third is a few miles lower down; but the canal having been staked at Santoo, I was prevented from examining it. Between Santoo and Chinkeang it passes through an undulating country; its breadth varying from 70 to 90 feet, the banks rising in many places from 30 to 40 feet, and its depth varying from 9 to 15 feet. It is in two places, near the south and west gates, contracted by stone buttresses to little more than 20 feet in width, and at the gates it is crossed by stone bridges, so that it is not navigable by large junks. Whether the branches below Santoo are so, I had not the opportunity of ascertaining. In forming it advantage has apparently been taken of the

line of the natural watercourses leading from the hills
to the river, but in many places the excavation must
have been a work of considerable labour. A small
branch of it, now blocked up and nearly filled up, passes
through the town of Chinkeang by means of water
gates.

The canal leading from the Yang-tse-keang to the
northward is a much larger and finer one. It has several very large branches communicating with the
river, besides numberless ramifications joining the
main channels. The main branch leading from Chinkeang has its principal mouth about a mile above
Golden Island, with another smaller one directly opposite the west end of the town. The latter passes
through the old town of Quatchow, now nearly all in
ruins; and from this town another small branch communicates with the river half a mile lower down. In
this neighbourhood the whole country to the northward
of the Yang-tse-keang is little if at all above the level
of the river, and is entirely laid out in paddy fields,
separated from the canals and ditches by embankments,
which form the only paths and roads. The main
branch of the canal is from 80 to 100 yards wide, with
a fine broad towing-path on the embankment separating
it from the paddy fields. It has five fathoms at its
entrance; and from the junks sunk in it to form the
barrier being covered by the water, I imagine carries
its depth up as far as I went. Its course is north a
little easterly; and about eight miles up there is a fine
pagoda called Sanshaho, where it is joined by another
large branch leading from E-ching-hien, a town on the
Yang-tse-keang, about 12 miles above Chinkeang. At
the point of junction it bends to the eastward for a

quarter of a mile, and then resumes it northerly course to the large and rich town of Yang-chow-foo, three miles above Sanshaho. Before turning to the north-ward again it is, I believe, joined by a third large branch, running into the Yang-tse-keang a mile below Silver Island; though I could not from the top of the pagoda see the junction, nor was I at the time aware of the existence of this branch. There is another large opening in the north bank of the river below Chinushau pagoda, which I think in all probability communicates also with this canal. At Sanshaho both the Chinkeang and E-ching branches were blocked up by barriers formed of sunken junks and stakes; and near the turn to the eastward there was a third barrier, which I imagine must have been at the junction of the Silver Island branch. There is a considerable village at Sanshaho, and a josshouse, now sadly gone to decay, but showing the remains of great splendour, and roofed with the Imperial yellow and green tiles. At this time the river was evidently much above its ordinary level, as not only were the peasants cutting the paddy up to their middles in water, but many of the villages and the houses in Quatchow, as well as the courts of this josshouse, had water in them. From what has been said above, it would require a large force to establish an efficient blockade of the canal on this side.

THE END.

LONDON:
Printed by A. SPOTTISWOODE,
New-Street-Square.

For EU product safety concerns, contact us at Calle de José Abascal, 56–1°, 28003 Madrid, Spain or eugpsr@cambridge.org.

www.ingramcontent.com/pod-product-compliance
Ingram Content Group UK Ltd.
Pitfield, Milton Keynes, MK11 3LW, UK
UKHW010338140625
459647UK00010B/688